awesome

awesome

JEN AGRESTA &
SARAH WASSNER FLYNN

8

NATIONAL
GEOGRAPHIC
KiDS

WASHINGTON, D.C.

HEY THERE, AWESOME READERS!

ARE YOU READY ...

... to behold the most amazing sights and scenes on our planet? Then you've come to the right place. But there's so much to show you ... where to start? How about we just take it from the top:

WHAT IS AWESOME 8?

Awesome 8 is a picture-packed list book of the absolutely coolest, weirdest, and craziest things we could think of. You know, things you totally have to see to believe.

WHY EIGHT?

Well, why not? There are top ten lists—and if you ask us, eight is a great number. Better than ten even, because that means the things on our list have to be even cooler to make the cut!

DO I HAVE TO START AT THE BEGINNING?

No way. This book was designed with you in mind. Pick up the book, flip to a page that interests you, and read away! Don't like a topic? Skip it. Love a topic? Read it twice!

WHAT ELSE IS IN THIS BOOK?

You mean besides a glimpse into everything the world has to offer? Okay, you got us—we threw in more: fun facts, clever captions, and even a few spreads where we take a deeper dive into some of the things and places featured ... because they're just too cool for two sentences.

WHAT AM I WAITING FOR?

We don't know! Turn the page, and happy reading!

TABLE OF CONTENTS

EIGHT
HAIR-RAISING
ROLLER COASTERS

BUCKLE UP AND HANG ON! HERE'S YOUR TICKET TO SOME OF THE WORLD'S STEEPEST, SCARIEST, AND CURVIEST COASTERS.

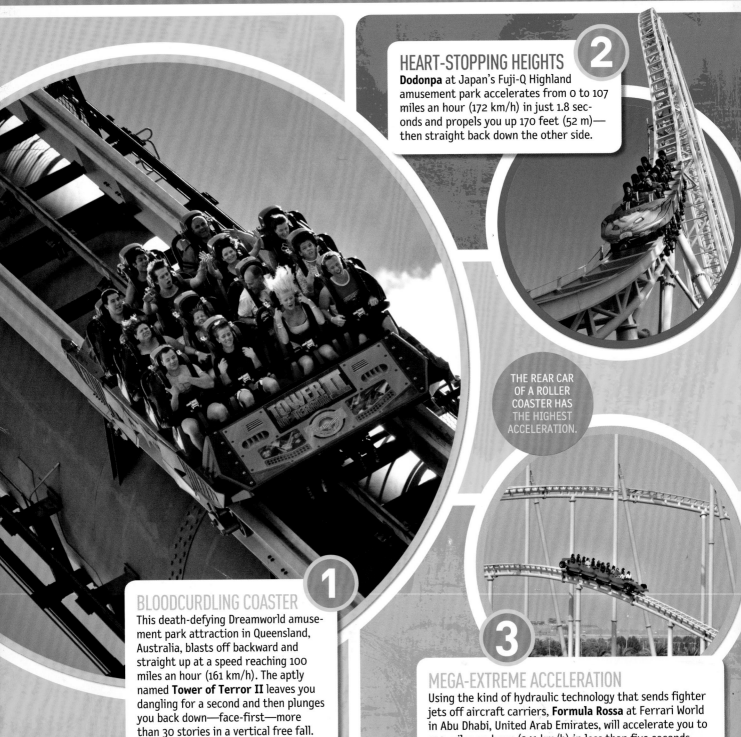

HEART-STOPPING HEIGHTS
2
Dodonpa at Japan's Fuji-Q Highland amusement park accelerates from 0 to 107 miles an hour (172 km/h) in just 1.8 seconds and propels you up 170 feet (52 m)—then straight back down the other side.

THE REAR CAR OF A ROLLER COASTER HAS THE HIGHEST ACCELERATION.

BLOODCURDLING COASTER
1
This death-defying Dreamworld amusement park attraction in Queensland, Australia, blasts off backward and straight up at a speed reaching 100 miles an hour (161 km/h). The aptly named **Tower of Terror II** leaves you dangling for a second and then plunges you back down—face-first—more than 30 stories in a vertical free fall.

MEGA-EXTREME ACCELERATION
3
Using the kind of hydraulic technology that sends fighter jets off aircraft carriers, **Formula Rossa** at Ferrari World in Abu Dhabi, United Arab Emirates, will accelerate you to 150 miles an hour (241 km/h) in less than five seconds.

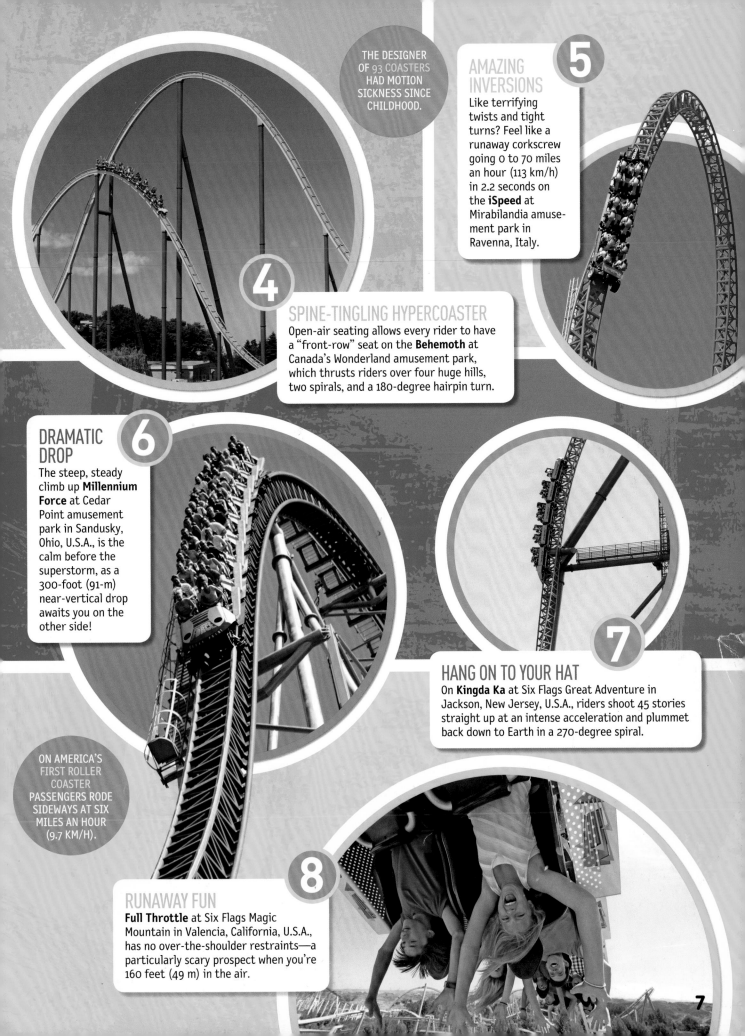

5

AMAZING INVERSIONS

Like terrifying twists and tight turns? Feel like a runaway corkscrew going 0 to 70 miles an hour (113 km/h) in 2.2 seconds on the **iSpeed** at Mirabilandia amusement park in Ravenna, Italy.

4

SPINE-TINGLING HYPERCOASTER

Open-air seating allows every rider to have a "front-row" seat on the **Behemoth** at Canada's Wonderland amusement park, which thrusts riders over four huge hills, two spirals, and a 180-degree hairpin turn.

6

DRAMATIC DROP

The steep, steady climb up **Millennium Force** at Cedar Point amusement park in Sandusky, Ohio, U.S.A., is the calm before the superstorm, as a 300-foot (91-m) near-vertical drop awaits you on the other side!

7

HANG ON TO YOUR HAT

On **Kingda Ka** at Six Flags Great Adventure in Jackson, New Jersey, U.S.A., riders shoot 45 stories straight up at an intense acceleration and plummet back down to Earth in a 270-degree spiral.

8

RUNAWAY FUN

Full Throttle at Six Flags Magic Mountain in Valencia, California, U.S.A., has no over-the-shoulder restraints—a particularly scary prospect when you're 160 feet (49 m) in the air.

EIGHT Remarkable RUINS

AT THESE AMAZING ARCHAEOLOGICAL SITES AROUND THE WORLD, EXPLORE CLUES TO UNLOCK THE WAYS ANCIENT PEOPLES LIVED, WORKED, AND WORSHIPPED.

1 SUPER-SCULPTURES

Averaging 14 tons (12.7 MT) and 13 feet (4 m) tall, **Easter Island's** 887 monumental head-and-torso sculptures were carved out of volcanic rock by Rapa Nui peoples more than 500 years ago. The human figures are thought to have been created to honor ancestors or other people important to these native Polynesian inhabitants.

2 MOUNTAIN MARVEL

One of the world's best-known and most-visited sites, **Machu Picchu** is an engineering marvel—a multilevel complex of temples, walls, homes, and connecting steps built by the Inca around 1450 in what is now Peru.

SOME STONE STRUCTURES AT MACHU PICCHU ARE FIT SO TIGHTLY EVEN A KNIFE BLADE CAN'T FIT BETWEEN THEM!

5 MONUMENTAL TEMPLE

Built in the fifth century B.C., the **Parthenon** was constructed from 22,000 tons (19,958 MT) of marble hauled from a mind-blowing distance of ten miles (16 km) away.

4 UNPARALLELED PYRAMIDS

The **Giza Pyramids** were built some 4,500 years ago as monumental tombs for Egyptian pharaohs. The Great Pyramid, largest of the three, is the only remaining member of the Seven Wonders of the Ancient World.

ANGKOR WAT IS SURROUNDED BY A 650-FOOT (200-M)-WIDE WATER-FILLED MOAT.

8 JAW-DROPPING COMPLEX

Dating back to the Khmer Empire in the 12th century, Cambodia's **Angkor Wat** is the largest religious monument ever built. Its sprawling 500-acre (202-ha) temple complex features gardens, canals, and other awe-inspiring structures.

7 SPECTACULAR SITE

The archaeological site of **Göbekli Tepe**, in Turkey, is home to what is believed to be the world's oldest known temple. More than 11,000 years ago, ancient peoples carved, moved, and arranged its massive, multi-ton limestone pillars.

3 SPLENDID STRUCTURES

Located in what is now the Hashemite Kingdom of Jordan, the sublime buildings of the ancient city of **Petra** were hand-carved into the face of immense sandstone cliffs some 2,000 years ago.

6 COLOSSAL COLOSSEUM

Ancient Rome's supersize stone amphitheater could seat about 50,000 people, who flocked to the four-story **Colosseum** to witness public events such as wild-animal battles and gruesome gladiator combat.

EIGHT Perilous

PREDATORS

① BEAR IT

The **grizzly bear**—which can weigh as much as a small car—is a speedy and stealthy hunter, preying on animals as tiny as mice and as large as moose. Supersharp curved claws help the bear trap prey while superstrong teeth tear its meal to shreds.

KNOCK OUT

2

Growing to be as long as a giraffe is tall, a giant **saltwater croc** has an appetite as big as its body. A "saltie" will snag its victim by first knocking it out with a powerful tail, and then dragging it underwater until it drowns.

DEADLY BLOW

4

A threatened **puffer fish** isn't just full of hot air: The long spikes that cover its ballooned body are extremely toxic to the touch. In fact, each fish contains enough toxins to kill 30 adult humans.

COLD AS ICE

5

In the Arctic, **polar bears** stalk seals as the seals emerge from the ice, relying on explosive speed and massive size to pounce on the prey before they know what hit them. With a little luck and one swift swipe of its sharp claws, a polar bear nabs a seal—a meal that provides up to eight days of energy for the bear.

POLAR BEARS NEED TO KILL UP TO 75 SEALS A YEAR TO SURVIVE.

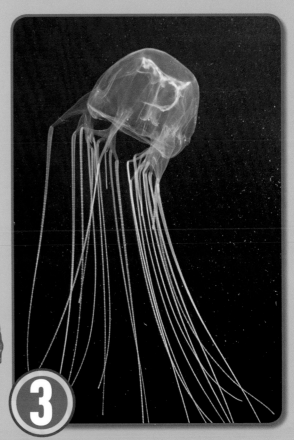

SHOCKING STING

3

Lethal doesn't always mean large: The **Australian box jellyfish,** whose bell is smaller than a basketball, stuns its prey with a deadly injection of venom. See one when you're out swimming? Head the other way—and quick: Its tentacles can stretch ten feet (3 m) in length, and just one sting can send you into shock.

TERROR TEAM

6

In a pride of **African lions,** it's the agile, fast females that do most of the hunting. Typically, lionesses team up to take down large prey, with one delivering a crushing bite to the neck while the others pounce for the feast.

TRUE COLORS

7

The bold colors on a **poison dart frog** tell potential predators to watch out! Tinier than a paper clip, this "blue jeans" frog—found in the rain forests of South America—oozes powerful poison through its skin.

FIERCE FORCE

8

Da na. Da na. Da na da na da na da na da naaahhhh ... A **great white shark's** 300 teeth slice into its prey like tiny steak knives, ripping its skin to shreds. The world's largest flesh-eating fish, this king of the predators bites with a force that's 20 times more powerful than a human jaw.

TURN THE PAGE FOR MORE COOL ANIMAL INFO!

WEIRD ANIMAL DEFENSES

A deadly bite. A stunning sting. A toxic injection that can paralyze you in an instant. These are just some of the ways that certain animals defend themselves. While every animal is somehow equipped to protect itself from danger as it finds food or guards its territory, some species have evolved unique—and even wacky—weapons that help make them extra-fearsome killers.

So what makes these animals so deadly? Check out the four formidable creatures on the opposite page to discover a few of the unrivaled powers some creatures possess.

PETS' DEFENSES, DECODED

If you have a pet, you've probably seen little Fluffy or Finnster act a little funny from time to time. He could be playing around—or some of his oddball behavior may be a way for him to tell you, "Hey, I'm scared" or "Watch out!" Here's how some of your pet's mysterious moves may actually be defense mechanisms.

Puffy Tail: Ever notice your cat's tail and fur standing on end? Your kitty is trying to give the impression that he's bigger than he really is. He may do this if he feels threatened—but plenty of cats puff up when they're playing, too.

Pulled-Back Ears: Your pooch's bark is the most obvious way to tell if he's upset, but pulled-back ears that are flat against the head also indicate that he's on high alert.

Fluttering Fins: If you have a few fish, you may spot one of them shaking or quivering her fins in front of a tank-mate. It's her way of showing the other fish who's boss.

THE ANIMAL:
Spanish ribbed newt
THE HABITAT: Spain, Portugal, and Morocco
THE WEAPON: Retractable ribs
FEARSOME FACT: When attacked, the Spanish ribbed newt shifts its ribs forward at an angle and pushes them through its stretched skin. The result? A row of spikes on both sides of its body that act like poisonous barbs.

THE ANIMAL: Secretary bird
THE HABITAT: Grasslands of central and southern Africa
THE WEAPON: Large feet and razor-sharp talons
FEARSOME FACT: This giant bird uses its long powerful legs and big feet to stomp its prey, like lizards, frogs, and snakes. It delivers a bone-crushing blow with each mighty step.

THE ANIMAL: Electric eel
THE HABITAT: The Amazon River in South America
THE WEAPON: Electricity
FEARSOME FACT: With electric organs running along the length of its body, these sneaky swimmers can stun unsuspecting prey with a shocking volt that's strong enough to knock a horse off its feet.

THE ANIMAL: Pangolin
THE HABITAT: Asia and sub-Saharan Africa
THE WEAPON: Spiky scales
FEARSOME FACTS: When threatened, these rare mammals curl into a supertight ball, with their scale-covered skin serving as a nearly impenetrable coat of armor. They also scare away enemies by lashing their spiky-edged tail.

BOAT IN THE SKY

1

This **hovercraft** glides over land and water, soaring up to 20 feet (6 m) in the air and reaching speeds that can surpass a speeding car. It can also skim over sand, swamps, and snow.

EIGHT
FANTASTIC FLIERS

ATTENTION, PASSENGERS: FEEL FREE TO ROAM ABOUT THE CABIN AS YOU EXPLORE SOME OF THE COOLEST CRAFTS EVER TO SOAR THE SKIES!

A COMPANY IS DEVELOPING A WINDOWLESS AIRPLANE WITH INTERIOR WALLS LINED WITH THIN SCREENS THAT WOULD PROJECT PANORAMIC VIEWS OF THE SKIES OUTSIDE IN REAL TIME.

DOUBLE TIME

2

Think of this **gyrocopter** as a convertible in the sky. With an open cockpit, the pilot and passenger of this tandem, two-seat, superlightweight 'copter are exposed to the elements, making for one wild ride.

D-MLTF

www.aeronautix.de

HELP FROM ABOVE

It's a parachute ... it's a plane ... it's a **paraplane!** This ultralight aircraft—attached to a parachute—relies on wind and a small motor to get air, gaining altitude as high as 10,000 feet (3 km).

3

DRIVE AND FLY

This car's got wings! Drive it to the local airport, press a button, and transform the vehicle from an **automobile into an airplane** in just 30 seconds. Zip down the runway and take off, hitting top flying speeds of 120 miles an hour (193 km/h).

4

5

RUNS ON THE SUN

Solar panels line nearly every inch of the **Solar Impulse** plane's wingspan, absorbing the sun's energy and storing it in batteries that can power the plane for more than 26 hours.

MULTITASKING

This funky flying machine is said to be the world's first "green" helicopter. Using electricity to take off, fly, and land, the lightweight **multicopter** has 16 rotors and can fly for about 20 minutes.

6

7

COOL ZOOM

Imagine not having to worry about being late for school ever again! The futuristic **Fly Citycopter** is still in concept stage, but this compact personal helicopter could someday be zipping across skies near you.

8

JET-SETTER

A Swiss pilot known as **"Fusion Man"** is the first to fly with jet fuel–powered wings strapped to his back. Leaping out of a plane from 8,000 feet (2,438 m) above the Earth, Fusion Man flies at a breakneck speed of more than 180 miles an hour (290 km/h), using his body to change position as he zips around.

15

EIGHT
STEEPEST SPORTS

EVER WONDERED WHAT IT WOULD BE LIKE TO SURF DOWN A VOLCANO OR WALK ALONG A THIN WIRE THOUSANDS OF FEET ABOVE GROUND? FIND OUT HOW SOME FEARLESS ATHLETES TAKE COMPETITION TO THE EXTREME.

1 WINGING IT
At the World BASE Race, competitors wear wing-suits to soar from steep cliffs. Free-falling faster than a speeding train for a period of about two minutes, **BASE jumpers** eventually pull a para-chute to glide gently to the ground.

IN THE SPORT OF BASE JUMPING, "BASE" STANDS FOR THE FOUR CATEGORIES OF OBJECTS OFF WHICH A PERSON JUMPS: BUILDING, ANTENNA, SPAN, EARTH.

2 WHEELS TO FLY
Rock and roll! A **free rider** soars over a steep rock wall in Moab, Utah, U.S.A. In free riding, cyclists use obstacles in nature—like rock formations and twisty trails—to perform daring tricks and stunts.

3 BALANCING ACT
No fear here! A daredevil tiptoes along a **narrow wire** on her way to crossing between two cliffs in the Italian Alps. Let's just hope she doesn't look down: A stumble at this height would be like falling from the top of the Empire State Building!

THROWN FOR A LOOP

Stunt cyclist Danny MacAskill seems to defy gravity by riding around a 16-foot (5-m)-tall loop-the-loop. Here, he's shown in a time-lapsed photo making a full revolution before riding away.

4

GO WITH THE FLOW

This sport is on fire! In **ash boarding**, you simply strap a wooden board on your feet and shoot down the lava, ash, and pebble slope of an active volcano, reaching speeds of up to 50 miles an hour (80 km/h).

5

CURVE APPEAL

Cars and motorcycles **drive sideways** in this dizzying display near Jammu, India. Thanks to centripetal force, vehicles stay stuck to the wall as they loop around the curved course.

6

7

BIG AIR

A snowboarder flies during the **slopestyle** event at the 2014 Winter Olympics in Sochi, Russia. In slopestyle, competitors race down a mountain dotted with obstacles, like ramps and rails, letting them catch major air. Good thing the snow provides a soft landing!

8

HIGH DIVE

CANNONBALL! A brave **diver** takes the plunge off the La Quebrada Cliffs in Acapulco, Mexico. The height of the jump? Some 150 feet (46 m)—four times taller than a platform diving board.

①

GOTTA GO!

A plumber in the U.K. built the **world's fastest functioning toilet.** Equipped with a motorbike engine hidden beneath the seat, this potty can pick up speeds topping 55 miles an hour (89 km/h)!

FURZE

EIGHT
ULTIMATE TOILETS

YOU MIGHT WANT TO SIT DOWN FOR THIS: FROM GOLDEN THRONES TO ANIMAL-INSPIRED URINALS, THESE FAR-OUT FLUSHERS ARE ABSOLUTELY FABULOUS.

②

OFF THE WALL

This mega-bathroom in Chongqing, China, contains about a thousand toilets—including dozens of **colorful urinals** in the shape of objects like toothy fish. Good thing those fish can't bite!

BLING IT ON

3

This **24-karat-gold toilet** brings major bling to this bathroom. The creation of a Hong Kong jeweler, the room cost some $3.5 million to build, earning it the title of the world's most expensive bathroom.

POP-UP POTTY

4

Now you see it ... now you don't! This **pop-up toilet**, found in some European cities, appears from underground when you need to use it—then automatically lowers out of sight when your, uh, business is done.

> ECO-FRIENDLY ELECTRIC TOILETS USE HEAT TO BURN HUMAN WASTE INTO ASH, WHICH YOU THEN THROW IN THE GARBAGE.

IN THE TANK

Part toilet, part aquarium—who knew the two would pair so swimmingly? And no need to worry about flushing your fish away: They're in a separate tank that doesn't empty so they can safely swim around.

5

LOO WITH A VIEW

6

Why, hello there! While taking a pit stop in this public toilet, you can **watch the world go by**, thanks to one-way glass that is see-through from the inside and a mirror on the outside. You can see passers-by—but they can only see themselves.

MICRO-FLUSHER

7

Now that's one **tiny toilet**! The world's smallest, in fact. Created in a lab using focused ion beam technology, this toilet is petite enough to easily fit on a strand of a spider's web.

HIGH-TECH TOILET

8

Once you take a seat on this **futuristic flusher**, you may not want to get up! The Numi is equipped with a heated seat, a foot warmer, and an automatic lid, and it will play your favorite tunes as you, um, tinkle.

RIGHTEOUS ROCK FORMATIONS

MOTHER NATURE IS A MASTER SCULPTOR! HERE ARE SOME OF HER MOST SPECTACULAR—AND MOST CURIOUS—CREATIONS.

ALIEN INVASION

2

Some compare it to the landscape of Mars! Fantastically eerie sandstone **"goblins"** mark the terrain of Goblin Valley State Park in Utah, U.S.A.

TEETER-TOTTER

1

Gravity? What gravity?! This narrow 29.5-foot (9-m)-tall **column of basalt** seems to balance perilously over St. Marys Bay in Nova Scotia, Canada.

STEEP AND SACRED

3

Rising 867 feet (264 m) from base to summit in northwest Wyoming, U.S.A., **Devils Tower** is a sacred site to a number of American Indian tribes.

MAJESTIC DESERT

4

Centuries of sand blown by desert winds have shaped amazing chalk-rock sculptures in the **White Desert** of Egypt.

GREAT GRANITE!

5

More than 500 million years of erosion by wind, rain, and seawater sculpted the unusually shaped **Remarkable Rocks** in Flinders Chase National Park on Kangaroo Island, South Australia.

COOL CURVES

6

Erosion sculpted the steep slopes and dramatic curves of this sandstone formation (called **"The Wave"**) in Vermilion Cliffs, a rugged 280,000-acre (113,312-ha) national monument in northern Arizona, U.S.A.

AMAZING ISLAND

7

Storm-wave erosion spanning thousands of years shaped **Turnip Rock,** a tree-covered rock island in Lake Huron, off the coast of Michigan, U.S.A.

DELICATE ARCH

8

This bending boulder is one of more than 2,000 documented **natural stone arches** in the high desert of Arches National Park, Utah, U.S.A.

EIGHT Wackiest WEATHER EVENTS

CHECK OUT THESE DANGEROUS AND DOWNRIGHT WEIRD METEOROLOGICAL PHENOMENA—FROM ICY COLD OCEAN DEPTHS TO FIERY HOT VOLCANOES ABOUT TO BLOW THEIR TOPS!

A MEGA-EXTREME WIND GUST OF 231 MILES AN HOUR (372 KM/H)—AS FAST AS CARS QUALIFYING FOR THE INDY 500—BLEW ACROSS THE SUMMIT OF MOUNT WASHINGTON, NEW HAMP-SHIRE, U.S.A., IN 1934.

1 ICY FINGERS

Brinicles form beneath sea ice when brine (salt) sinks rapidly below the surface. As it descends, the water around it freezes in an icy sheath that, upon touching the seafloor, encases any unfortunate creatures in its path in a web of ice.

DUST STORMS

These giant, swirling, advancing **walls of dust** and debris often arrive without warning. A 2009 dust storm in Australia was so big it was visible from space!

RAINING FISH

Strong, swirling winds can suck **fish** (and sometimes even frogs!) out of shallow water and into a storm cloud, where they are carried for sometimes long distances before being "rained" out.

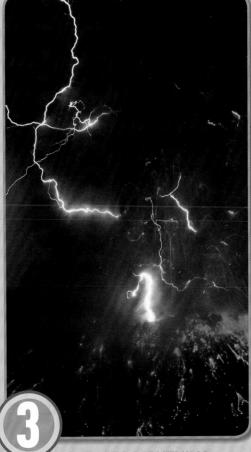

VOLCANIC LIGHTNING

Also called a **"dirty thunderstorm,"** this phenomenon occurs when electrical bolts accompany the exploding ash and lava of a volcanic eruption.

LIGHTNING CAN CONTAIN 100 MILLION ELECTRICAL VOLTS.

FIRE TORNADOES

Hot, dry air from raging wildfires can rise quickly and form a **"firewhirl"**— a 2-foot (0.6-m)-wide spinning vortex of burning debris, embers, combustible gases, and ash that can reach 100 feet (30.5 m) high.

RED SPRITES, BLUE JETS

Split-second lightning that occurs above active thunderstorms, **sprites** are reddish electrical bursts, and **jets** are bright cones of light that shoot up from the tops of thunderclouds.

ICE BOMBS

Hailstones are lumps or balls of ice that can rain down during thunderstorms and cause severe damage and injury. Some reaching 3.1 inches (8 cm) in diameter have even put fist-size holes in car windows!

SLIDING STONES

Stones that seem to move on their own? Scientists puzzled over these **remarkable rocks** in Death Valley, California, U.S.A., for many years before learning the awesome truth.

TURN THE PAGE TO DISCOVER HOW!

MYSTERY SOLVED!

Sailing Stones in Death Valley

SO, WHAT TOOK SO LONG?

Why did it take half a century or more for scientists to figure out what was moving the stones? Several factors make observing them in action difficult to near impossible.

Location: Racetrack Playa sits more than 3,600 feet (1,100 m) above sea level and is a three-hour drive from the closest town.

Occurrence: The moving rocks are a rare phenomenon. Because the playa is dry the vast majority of the time, it could be a decade or longer before there is enough rain to make a pond deep enough to form the ice that pushes the rocks and, thus, create new trails—trails that form out of sight in the soft mud underneath the floating ice.

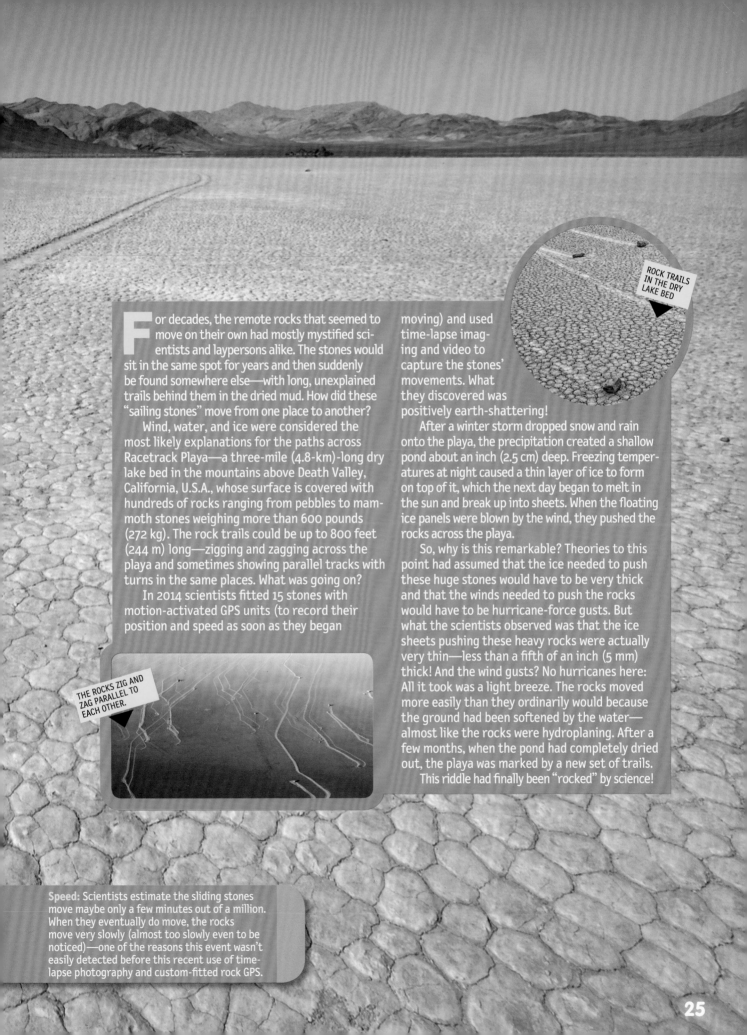

For decades, the remote rocks that seemed to move on their own had mostly mystified scientists and laypersons alike. The stones would sit in the same spot for years and then suddenly be found somewhere else—with long, unexplained trails behind them in the dried mud. How did these "sailing stones" move from one place to another?

Wind, water, and ice were considered the most likely explanations for the paths across Racetrack Playa—a three-mile (4.8-km)-long dry lake bed in the mountains above Death Valley, California, U.S.A., whose surface is covered with hundreds of rocks ranging from pebbles to mammoth stones weighing more than 600 pounds (272 kg). The rock trails could be up to 800 feet (244 m) long—zigging and zagging across the playa and sometimes showing parallel tracks with turns in the same places. What was going on?

In 2014 scientists fitted 15 stones with motion-activated GPS units (to record their position and speed as soon as they began moving) and used time-lapse imaging and video to capture the stones' movements. What they discovered was positively earth-shattering!

ROCK TRAILS IN THE DRY LAKE BED

After a winter storm dropped snow and rain onto the playa, the precipitation created a shallow pond about an inch (2.5 cm) deep. Freezing temperatures at night caused a thin layer of ice to form on top of it, which the next day began to melt in the sun and break up into sheets. When the floating ice panels were blown by the wind, they pushed the rocks across the playa.

So, why is this remarkable? Theories to this point had assumed that the ice needed to push these huge stones would have to be very thick and that the winds needed to push the rocks would have to be hurricane-force gusts. But what the scientists observed was that the ice sheets pushing these heavy rocks were actually very thin—less than a fifth of an inch (5 mm) thick! And the wind gusts? No hurricanes here: All it took was a light breeze. The rocks moved more easily than they ordinarily would because the ground had been softened by the water—almost like the rocks were hydroplaning. After a few months, when the pond had completely dried out, the playa was marked by a new set of trails.

This riddle had finally been "rocked" by science!

THE ROCKS ZIG AND ZAG PARALLEL TO EACH OTHER.

Speed: Scientists estimate the sliding stones move maybe only a few minutes out of a million. When they eventually do move, the rocks move very slowly (almost too slowly even to be noticed)—one of the reasons this event wasn't easily detected before this recent use of time-lapse photography and custom-fitted rock GPS.

CUTEST CRITTERS

THESE ANIMALS MAY BE SMALL IN SIZE, BUT THEY'RE PRETTY BIG ON AWESOME. HERE ARE EIGHT OF THE TINIEST (AND MOST ADORABLE!) CREATURES ON EARTH. SAY *AWW!*

1 DOGGONE ADORABLE

Considered by many to be the "cutest dog in Japan," **Shunsuke** the Pomeranian has thousands of followers on several social networking sites and two books featuring snaps of the photogenic pooch. Now that's one popular pup!

2 CUB LOVE

A **polar bear cub** is about the size of an ice-cream sandwich when it's born. But it doesn't take long for these cubs to get chubby: Relying on its mom's nutrient-rich milk, a cub can gain more than 30 pounds (13.6 kg) in a matter of months.

EYE SPY

What are you looking at? A **baby tarsier** shows off its huge peepers, which are about the same size and weight as its brain. Found exclusively in the islands of Southeast Asia, the nocturnal primate has the biggest eyes in the animal kingdom compared to its body size.

4

WHAT A DOLL

3

Boo the baby orangutan cuddles with a fuzzy stuffed animal. Considered to be one of the most intelligent land animals, orangutans in captivity tote toys around their habitat, stack giant Legos, and even play video games. Sound like anyone you know?

PETITE AND PRICKLY

5

A **pygmy hedgehog** pauses to lick its chops. Native to Africa, this pint-size, spiky mammal—the smallest of the 15 species of hedgehogs—can easily slip into a coffee cup!

MONKEYING AROUND

7

Future flutist? A **baby baboon** appears to be pretending to play an instrument with a stick. This baboon may be small now, but it will eventually grow to be one of the world's largest monkeys.

YOU CAN VISIT BABY PANDAS AT A BREEDING AND RESEARCH CENTER IN CHINA, WHERE 14 CUBS WERE ONCE BORN IN A SPAN OF THREE MONTHS.

UP A TREE

6

A **three-toed sloth** looks completely content relaxing on a branch. In the wild, these slow-moving mammals spend almost their entire lives in the rain forest canopy, coming down about once a week to use the bathroom.

PANDA-MONIUM

8

This pack of **panda cubs** heads out for playtime at the Wolong National Nature Reserve in China. Born in captivity, the cubs are cared for by their mothers with the help of specially trained experts as an effort to boost the dwindling population of pandas in China.

PHENOMENAL FOSSILS

TAKE A TRIP IN A GEOLOGICAL TIME MACHINE! FOSSILS REVEAL PLANTS AND ANIMALS FROM THE PAST.

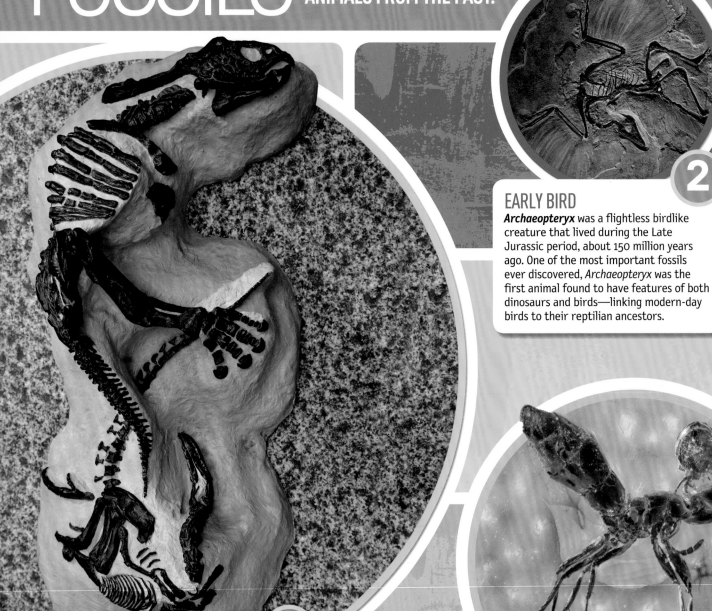

2 EARLY BIRD

Archaeopteryx was a flightless birdlike creature that lived during the Late Jurassic period, about 150 million years ago. One of the most important fossils ever discovered, *Archaeopteryx* was the first animal found to have features of both dinosaurs and birds—linking modern-day birds to their reptilian ancestors.

1 DEADLY DINO FIGHT

The 68-million-year-old well-preserved skeletons of a **Tyrannosaurus rex** and a **Triceratops** locked in battle showed that each had died from wounds inflicted by the other—with some of the *T. rex*'s teeth even found in the *Triceratops*'s skull!

3 STICKY SITUATION

Fossilized mites are hard to find. Luckily for scientists, this parasitic arachnid got stuck in tree resin—which eventually fossilized into amber—while it was attached to the head of the ant it was attacking.

5

RHINO SKULL

Streaming ash and rock from a volcanic eruption 9.2 million years ago in what is now Turkey "baked" and preserved this **rhino's skull and jaw.** Because the intense heat usually incinerates them, mammal fossils are rarely found in volcanic rock.

4

ASTOUNDING ARTHROPOD

This 520-million-year-old sea creature—called a **fuxhian-huiid**—is one of the earliest animal fossils ever found. Its discovery may help scientists learn more about the evolution of arthropods, such as insects and crustaceans.

TEETH **DATING BACK** 60,000–120,000 **YEARS MAY BE FOSSILS OF AN UNKNOWN SPECIES OF EARLY HUMAN.**

6

TERRIBLE TEETH

These fossilized teeth—yes, these are *teeth*—filled the entire lower jaw of the 270-million-year-old fish **Helicoprion.** The prehistoric creature didn't have any upper chompers—perhaps not needed when your lower ones work like a circular saw.

7

MONSTER FISH

These giant jaws spanning 11 feet (3.4 m) across and almost 9 feet (2.7 m) tall belonged to the prehistoric shark ***Megalodon***—a 50-foot (16-m), 55-ton (50-MT) predator that roamed the seas, munching on dolphins and baleen whales.

8

PREHISTORIC POOP

Researchers discovered **fossilized feces** (or "coprolites") marked with bite marks from a prehistoric shark. They believe the poop—possibly belonging to a crocodilian—was still inside the animal when it was nipped by the shark.

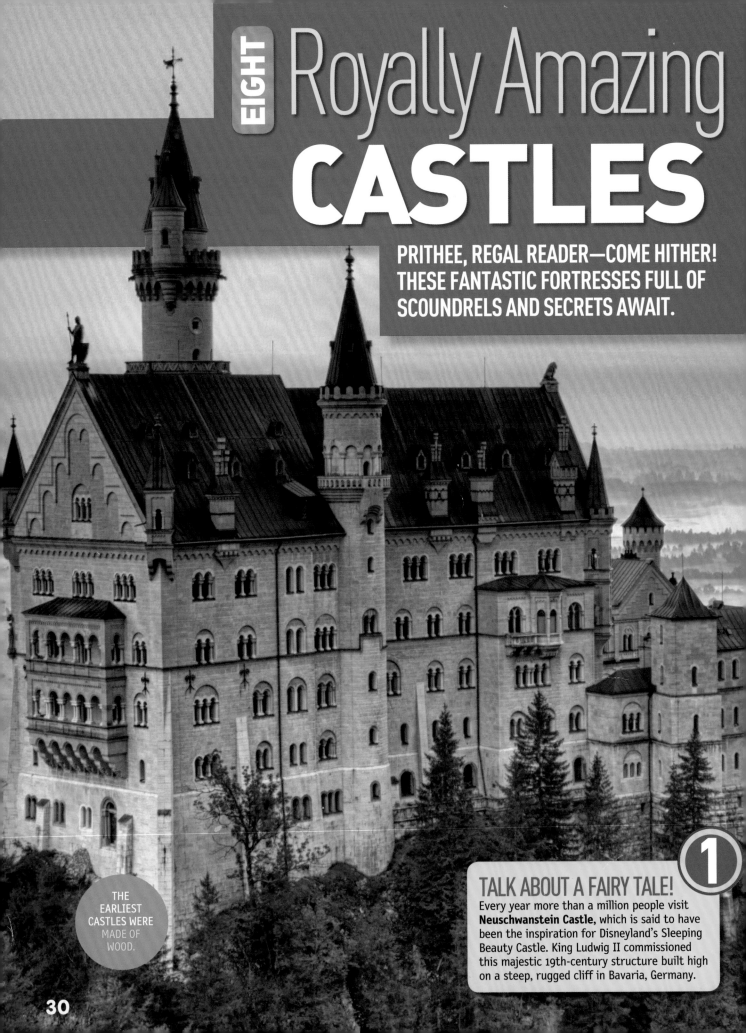

Royally Amazing
CASTLES

PRITHEE, REGAL READER—COME HITHER! THESE FANTASTIC FORTRESSES FULL OF SCOUNDRELS AND SECRETS AWAIT.

THE EARLIEST CASTLES WERE MADE OF WOOD.

① TALK ABOUT A FAIRY TALE!

Every year more than a million people visit **Neuschwanstein Castle,** which is said to have been the inspiration for Disneyland's Sleeping Beauty Castle. King Ludwig II commissioned this majestic 19th-century structure built high on a steep, rugged cliff in Bavaria, Germany.

TIME CAPSULE ②

Walk the paths walked by medieval knights and princesses! Visitors to the 14th-century moated **Bodiam Castle** in East Sussex, England, journey back in time as they explore the ruins and remaining interior rooms of this fantastic former fortification.

CASTLES WERE FIRST BUILT FOR DEFENSE AND AS A PLACE TO LAUNCH ATTACKS.

NATIONAL TREASURE ④

Founded in the ninth century, **Prague Castle** is a significant monument in the Czech Republic. The World Heritage site is also the largest ancient castle in the world, with an area of more than 750,000 square feet (69,677 sq m) containing gardens, palaces, and buildings.

WINGED WONDER ⑤

The look of **Himeji-jo,** the largest castle in Japan, has been likened to a white heron spreading its wings. Dating back to the 14th century, the 83-building complex is also a designated World Heritage site.

FIT FOR A BOY WIZARD ③

This 900-year-old castle in Northumberland, England, was the site of Harry's first flying lesson at Hogwarts in the film *Harry Potter and the Sorcerer's Stone.* Take flight like a Quidditch Keeper and sign up for broomstick training lessons on your next visit to **Alnwick Castle!**

FIERCE FORTRESS ⑥

For more than 900 years this castle looming above Austria's Salzachtal Valley and surrounded by mountains has survived numerous sieges and attacks. **Hohenwerfen Fortress** was also featured in the 1965 film *The Sound of Music.*

ABIDE THE TIDE ⑦

A medieval island-abbey perched majestically in northwestern France, **Mont Saint-Michel** is surrounded by water at high tide and an expanse of sand and mud at low tide.

BRAN CASTLE ⑧

More than half a million visitors a year make their way to this Transylvanian destination also known as **"Dracula's Castle."** Does that nickname have any teeth to it?

TURN THE PAGE TO FIND OUT!

31

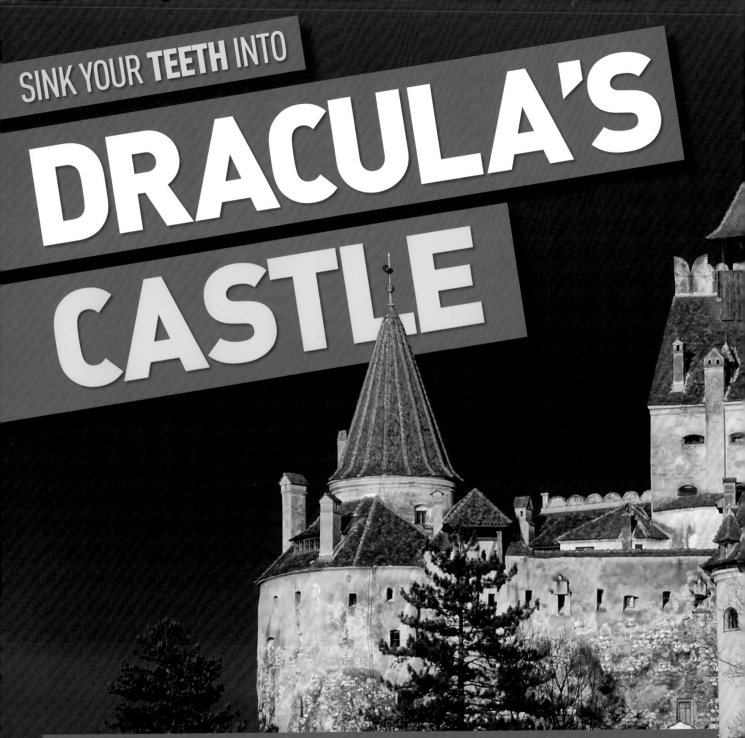

SINK YOUR TEETH INTO

DRACULA'S CASTLE

Though Bran Castle is commonly called "Dracula's Castle," the author who penned the famous vampire tale never actually set foot in this Romanian hilltop fortress. Once a medieval stronghold, later a royal residence, and now a popular tourist destination, Bran Castle is one of a few castles that is thought to have provided inspiration for Irish novelist Bram Stoker's *Dracula*. Completed in the 14th century, Bran Castle initially served as a customs station for goods traveling in and out of Transylvania and as fortification in the effort to halt the expansion of the Ottoman Empire.

Stoker crafted his 1897 tale of the undead by researching the region and its folklore, which had long included vampire legends. The book's chief bloodsucker, Count Dracula, is thought to have been influenced by an actual person:

15th-century military leader Vlad III, Prince of Wallachia (son of Vlad Dracul, or "Dráculea"), who Stoker likely came upon in his research. Depicted in some historical texts as a bloodthirsty warrior and vividly referred to as "Vlad the Impaler," the prince doesn't actually have a whole lot in common with the fictional character who Stoker bestowed with his name. And although warriors and royalty have indeed occupied the soaring structure on a steep cliff over the centuries, there's no evidence that the monarch—and national hero for many Romanians—ever made his home at Bran Castle.

Still, visitors to Bran today can get a taste of the famous fictional fanged count. Explore the dungeon, descend the secret staircase, and ride a glass elevator to experience "Dracula's escape route"—until dark, that is ...

LEGENDARY LINEUP

NAME: Vampire
ALIAS: Prince of Darkness
WANTED FOR: Feeding off the blood of humans
MOST DANGEROUS: At night
FEAR(S): Daylight, garlic, stakes

NAME: Werewolf
ALIAS: Lycanthrope
WANTED FOR: Attacking humans
MOST DANGEROUS: During a full moon
FEAR(S): Silver bullets

NAME: Kraken
ALIAS: Sea Mischief
WANTED FOR: Capsizing ships, terrorizing the seas
MOST DANGEROUS: In the ocean
FEAR(S): Washing up on a beach

NAME: Krampus
ALIAS: Christmas Devil
WANTED FOR: Swatting naughty children with birch sticks and taking them to the underworld
MOST DANGEROUS: In December
FEAR(S): Well-behaved kids

33

Funky TREE HOUSES

THESE HOMES-AWAY-FROM-HOME TAKE THE TRADITIONAL TREE HOUSE TO A WHOLE NEW LEVEL.

2 COCOON TREE

Know what it feels like to be a butter-fly! These **floating aluminum pods** are covered with a waterproof tarp and are rigged to hang between trees. They can be customized and special ordered at a starting cost of around $8,000.

A MINISTER IN TENNESSEE, U.S.A., BUILT A 10,000-SQUARE-FOOT (929-SQ-M), FIVE-STORY TREE HOUSE CONTAINING 80 ROOMS, A CHURCH, AND A BELL TOWER.

1 LOFTY POD

The Redwoods Treehouse **wraps around the trunk of a redwood** tree north of Auckland, New Zealand. Sitting more than 30 feet (10 m) high and acces-sible via an ele-vated walkway, the cocoon-like retreat can be rented out for parties and other events.

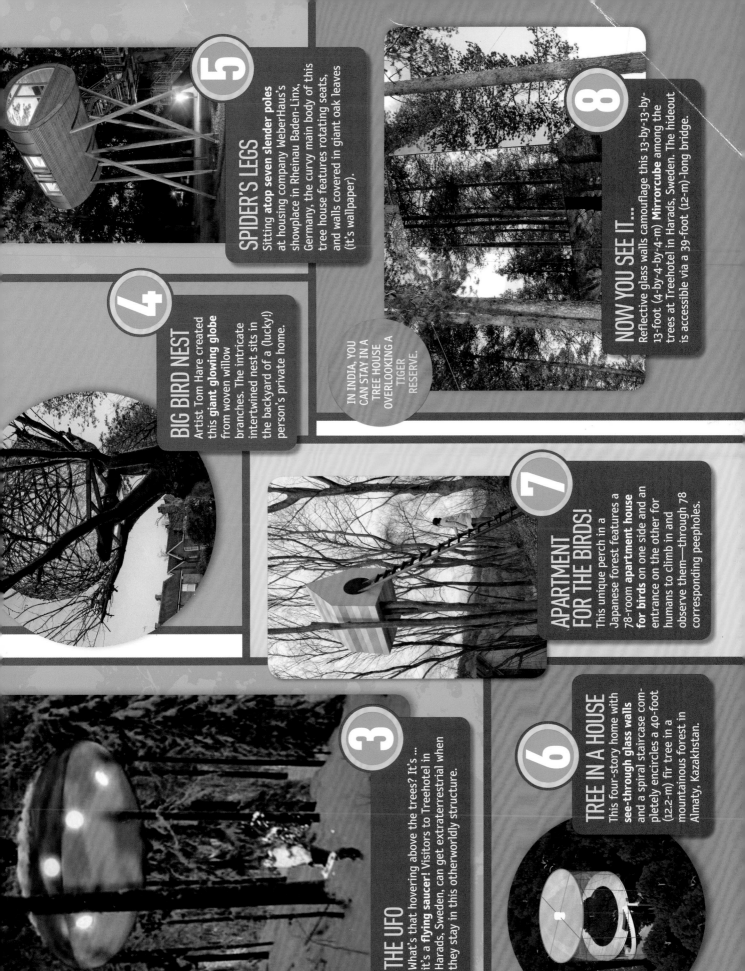

5 SPIDER'S LEGS

Sitting **atop seven slender poles** at housing company WeberHaus's showplace in Rheinau Baden-Linx, Germany, the curvy main body of this tree house features rotating seats, and walls covered in giant oak leaves (it's wallpaper).

8 NOW YOU SEE IT...

Reflective glass walls camouflage this 13-by-13-by-13-foot (4-by-4-by-4-m) **Mirrorcube** among the trees at Treehotel in Harads, Sweden. The hideout is accessible via a 39-foot (12-m)-long bridge.

IN INDIA, YOU CAN STAY IN A TREE HOUSE OVERLOOKING A TIGER RESERVE.

4 BIG BIRD NEST

Artist Tom Hare created this **giant glowing globe** from woven willow branches. The intricate intertwined nest sits in the backyard of a (lucky!) person's private home.

7 APARTMENT FOR THE BIRDS!

This unique perch in a Japanese forest features a 78-room **apartment house for birds** on one side and an entrance on the other for humans to climb in and observe them—through 78 corresponding peepholes.

3 THE UFO

What's that hovering above the trees? It's ... it's a **flying saucer!** Visitors to Treehotel in Harads, Sweden, can get extraterrestrial when they stay in this otherworldly structure.

6 TREE IN A HOUSE

This four-story home with **see-through glass walls** and a spiral staircase completely encircles a 40-foot (12.2-m) fir tree in a mountainous forest in Almaty, Kazakhstan.

1

UP AND AWAY!
Hundreds of balloons take to the sky in New Mexico, U.S.A., every October at the **Albuquerque International Balloon Fiesta,** the largest ballooning event on Earth.

THE FIRST MANNED HOT-AIR BALLOON FLIGHT TOOK PLACE IN FRANCE IN 1783.

EIGHT
WILD WORLD FESTIVALS
LIKE TO DANCE, GET MESSY, OR JUST FLOAT AWAY? THERE'S A PARTY OUT THERE FOR YOU!

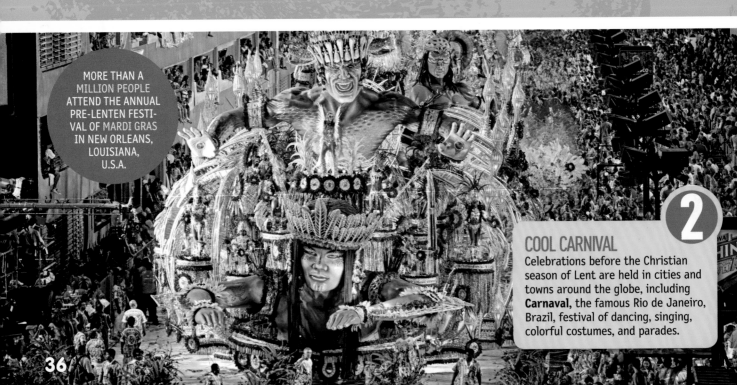

MORE THAN A MILLION PEOPLE ATTEND THE ANNUAL PRE-LENTEN FESTIVAL OF MARDI GRAS IN NEW ORLEANS, LOUISIANA, U.S.A.

2

COOL CARNIVAL
Celebrations before the Christian season of Lent are held in cities and towns around the globe, including **Carnaval,** the famous Rio de Janeiro, Brazil, festival of dancing, singing, colorful costumes, and parades.

DIA DE LOS MUERTOS

Every November, **Day of the Dead** celebrations in Mexico and throughout Latin America (and elsewhere, including parts of the U.S.A.) honor and remember departed loved ones through music, dancing, and sweets.

3

FESTIVAL OF COLORS

Participants throw brightly colored powders at each other during **Holi,** a Hindu religious festival celebrating the beginning of spring that has become popular with millions of people all over the world.

5

FIERY GOOD TIME

The annual daylong **Up Helly Aa** festival celebrating Shetland, Scotland, history ends with hundreds of costume-clad participants marching through town with torches and burning a full-scale replica of a Viking galley (longship).

6

FROSTY FUN

The **International Ice and Snow Festival** in Harbin, China, features giant sculptures carved out of snow and intricate, full-size buildings made from blocks of ice and illuminated by brightly colored lights.

7

FOOD FIGHT

Every August in Buñol, Spain, thousands of people gather to hurl more than 110 tons (100 MT) of overripe tomatoes at each other during **La Tomatina** festival.

TOMATO ACIDS CAN HELP CLEAR UP PIMPLES.

8

MUDDY PARTY

More than two million people head to Boryeong, South Korea, every summer for the small beach town's **Mud Festival,** in which participants wrestle, slide, and wade in mud from the area's mudflats—considered mineral-rich and beneficial to the skin.

EIGHT DELECTABLE DESSERTS

TAKE A BITE OUT OF THESE OVER-THE-TOP TREATS. FROM COLOSSAL WEDDING CAKES TO DELUXE DOUGHNUTS, THESE DESSERTS DO MORE THAN JUST SATISFY YOUR SWEET TOOTH.

1 GOING TO THE DOGS

To mark the royal wedding between the Duke and Duchess of Cambridge, a chef whipped up this **colossal (and dog-friendly!) confection** in the shape of Queen Elizabeth's prized pooches.

2 ICE CREAM CHIC

The $25,000 **Frrrozen Hot Chocolate sundae**—served exclusively at a New York City restaurant—sparkles with flecks of edible 24-karat gold. There's an even sweeter reward at the bottom of the bowl: a diamond bracelet!

3 BROWNIE BLISS

How to make the **world's most expensive brownie?** Sprinkle it with gold dust, and add a dash of hazelnuts imported from Italy. That's what you can order at a restaurant in Atlantic City, New Jersey, U.S.A., to the tune of $1,000—or the price of about 350 boxes of brownie mix.

4 CREAM OF THE CROP

Holy cannoli! This is one colossal cream-filled tube. Pastry chefs from a bakery in Boston, Massachusetts, U.S.A., whipped up the **world's largest cannoli,** measuring over seven feet (2.1 m) long and tipping the scales at 262.5 pounds (119 kg).

5 SPARKLY SWEET

Designed by a jeweler in Glasgow, Scotland, this **pink-frosting-topped cupcake** is "iced" with 12 tiny, twinkling diamonds. Worth more than $150,000, it's almost too pretty to eat!

A RESTAURANT IN SCOTLAND SERVES UP A RHUBARB-FLAVORED DESSERT FEATURING EDIBLE 24-KARAT GOLD LEAF AND VANILLA BEANS IMPORTED FROM MADAGASCAR.

7 WELL ROUNDED

Here's a doughnut flavor you don't taste every day: **SPAM!** In honor of National Doughnut Day, a restaurant in Lancashire, U.K., sandwiched the iconic ham-in-a-can inside a glazed doughnut, then deep-fried it for a crispy bite. Um, yum?!

6 A DIAMOND ON TOP

One British restaurant's **pricey pudding** costs more than a new car! The decadent details? Edible gold, champagne caviar, Belgian chocolate—and a two-carat diamond to take home after you've tasted every last morsel.

8 SUPERSLICE

It sounds like a pie-in-the-sky idea, but when 40 cooks in China set out to create the **world's largest pumpkin pie,** they did just that. Slices of the pie, which was wider than two king-size beds and weighed as much as a rhino, were served to guests at an amusement park.

SOUND THE TRUMPETS!
These low-pitched telescopic trumpets, called *dung chen,* are played in Tibetan Buddhist religious rituals and can reach lengths of more than ten feet (3 m).

THE WORLD'S OLDEST-KNOWN INSTRUMENTS ARE BELIEVED TO BE 40,000-YEAR-OLD BIRD-BONE-AND-MAMMOTH-IVORY FLUTES FOUND IN A CAVE IN GERMANY.

EIGHT
INCREDIBLE INSTRUMENTS
CHECK OUT SOME OF THE MOST ASTOUNDING SOUNDMAKING MARVELS EVER TO CARRY A TUNE.

2

LIGHT SHOW
When musicians move their hands across the **laser harp's** beams of light, the "break" in a beam sends commands to an electronic device such as a synthesizer, which produces the notes and different sounds.

UNUSUAL ORGAN **4**
Pipes attached to the seawall are connected to pipes inside the body of the **High Tide Organ,** a 49-foot (15-m)-tall sculpture in Blackpool, England. When the ocean's high tide rolls in, it pushes air pressure up the pipes and creates the sculpture's unique music.

SUPERSAX **5**
Stretching more than six feet (1.8 m) long and weighing 45 pounds (20.4 kg) or more, the **contrabass saxophone** is one of the biggest woodwind instruments around.

SUPERSTRING **3**
Featuring 4 necks, 2 sound holes, and 42 strings, the **Pikasso Guitar** was custom-made for musician Pat Metheny. It took two years (about 1,000 hours!) to build.

AQUEOUS INSTRUMENT **7**
Players of the **hydraulophone** produce sounds by using their fingers to block the flow of water coming through its holes. Stopping water through a particular hole creates a particular sound.

6 WOODEN WONDER
Created by the Mangbetu peoples of the Democratic Republic of the Congo, this five-string **Mangbetu harp** features a finely carved representation of a human head at the top of its long, curved neck.

TREE SONG **8**
When winds blow through the galvanized steel pipes of the **Singing Ringing Tree,** a twisting, treelike ten-foot (3-m)-tall musical sculpture in Lancashire, England, they create a hum of notes that span multiple octaves.

FAR-OUT FASHIONS

FORGET T-SHIRTS AND JEANS. IN THE SOMETIMES WACKY WORLD OF HIGH FASHION, CLOTHES ARE CONSIDERED A WORK OF ART. HERE ARE EIGHT OF THE WEIRDEST THINGS PEOPLE HAVE EVER WORN.

2 FRUIT ON THE BOTTOM

These **shoes are sweet**—down to your feet! These heels, designed by a Japanese artist, look almost good enough to eat. Just don't really try to snack on these shoes: Those sugary treats are totally fake.

1 BEACHY KEEN

Need a new look for the summer? Consider this **blue-hued style,** which brings new meaning to hair "waves." Surf's up—and so is your 'do!

3 FOR THE BIRDS

An employee of the company that crafts Angry Birds (also the wife of the creator) shows her support for the popular video game by walking the red carpet at a gala in this **animated gown.** What's next, a Minecraft tuxedo?

5 WORK IT
A model walks the runway in an out-there outfit by a Dutch designer who uses techniques like embroidery, illustrations, and photo collage to create his **ultra-eccentric looks.** Just shows that anything goes in the fashion world!

4 THROUGH THE LENS
Slip on these **silly-looking spectacles**—featured on the runway during Paris Fashion Week—and you just may see the world in a funkier light.

6 HAIR APPARENT
Talk about camera shy: A pop singer strikes a mysterious pose by hiding behind a **wall of blond hair.** We just have to wonder: Is she smiling underneath those strands?

7 PROPER TOPPERS
The **bigger the hat**—the better? At least that's the case at a horse race in Ascot, England, where funky fascinators—like these featuring an Olympic torch and soccer pitch—are a must.

8 FACE-OFF
Competitions over **funky facial hair** get fierce at the World Beard and Moustache Championships. Contestants like Mike Johnson prep for months to mold their mustaches and beards into masterpieces.

YOU CAN BUY BLUE JEANS MADE OUT OF RECYCLED WATER BOTTLES.

43

Extreme

TALK ABOUT DREAM JOBS! NAIL-BITING ADVENTURES AND AMAZING OPPORTUNITIES ARE ALL PART OF THE JOB IN THESE UBER-INTENSE AND DOWNRIGHT COOL CAREERS.

OCCUPATIONS

①

EYE OF THE STORM

Instead of ducking for cover when a tornado touches down, **storm chasers** head to the center of the system to track weather patterns and figure out what causes the funnels to form.

UP IN SMOKE

When a forest fire takes over remote, hard-to-reach areas, **smoke jumpers** will parachute out of a plane to fight the blaze from the ground. They face high winds and steep terrain—all while toting heavy equipment dropped down separately before the jump.

UNDER PRESSURE

Saturation divers live in a pressurized chamber for up to 28 days so they can withstand diving to depths of up to 1,000 feet (305 m) to recover black boxes from airplane crashes, repair oil wells, or do other underwater work.

SQUEEZE PLAY

How many ways can you milk a snake? Just ask a **venom milker**, who carefully collects poisonous fluid from a snake's fangs, usually by squeezing its head. Milkers then sell the venom for medical use.

TAKING THE HEAT

When a blaze takes over a wooded area, **forest firefighters** spring into action, dashing in to battle the flames with a hose. Crews sometimes have to walk for miles with heavy packs on their backs to reach the wildfire.

WIPED OUT

High-flying **window washers** brave frightening heights to keep skyscrapers sparkly clean. And this is no quick job: It can take up to three weeks to completely clean a 65-story building.

DEEP FREEZE

Researchers at the Concordia Station in Antarctica work in one of the coldest and most desolate places on Earth. In the winter, they'll do their work in darkness because the sun doesn't rise above the horizon for six straight months.

ROCK STAR

This is one explosive occupation! **Volcanologists** get up close and personal with active volcanoes. Observing things like lava flow and rock formations on volcanoes—and from a helicopter above—helps to determine why one erupts, and when it'll blow next.

TURN THE PAGE TO DISCOVER MORE!

MEET A VOLCANOLOGIST

John Stevenson studies volcanoes for a living. Here, he shares details on his extreme job.

PLUME RISING FROM A VOLCANO

SCIENCE-MINDED "As a kid, I really liked science and nature, and in college I pursued chemical engineering but studied geology as well. Having a background in all of the sciences gave me a better understanding of the bigger picture, from volcano monitoring to understanding eruptions."

BIG DIG "I once spent ten days collecting pumice and ash samples from a 4,200-year-old eruption in Iceland. We'd dig in the soil until we found the layer of ash that we wanted, then spend up to two hours photographing and taking samples. At night, we'd find a nice spot by a stream, eat dinner, and camp out."

DANGER IN THE AIR "Being exposed to the edge of a lava flow can be dangerous. The air is hot and can be thick with poisonous sulfur dioxide gas. Once, while working at the active Bárðarbunga volcano in Iceland, we had to wear gas masks and use an electronic gas meter as dust swirled around us."

RAINING ASH "When I worked at Volcán de Colima in Mexico, we camped a few miles from the crater. One night, I woke up to a whooshing sound. This quickly changed to a *patter-patter-patter* that sounded like heavy rain falling on the tent. When I put my hand out to feel the rain, it was covered in coarse grey sand. The volcano had erupted, and ash was raining down on us. We quickly packed up our stuff and headed to a safer spot."

JOB PERKS "I get to play with fun gadgets in cool locations. If I didn't have to work, I would still go hiking and camping and play with gadgets and computers in my spare time anyway. I enjoy trying to solve the problems of getting the right data and finding a way to process it so that it can tell us about how the world works."

WORKING IN THE FIELD

MY SCARIEST MOMENT!

"To get to a volcano observatory, we often have to drive along steep, twisty tracks. One time, the brakes of my pickup failed, and I went careening down a hill with no way of stopping. Fortunately, I managed to get around a bend and make it to a flatter spot so the truck could slow. If this had happened higher up, we would have had to choose between driving off the edge or into a tree. More volcanologists are killed getting to and from the volcanoes than by the volcanoes themselves."

Deadly DINOS

SIZE, SPEED, BITES, AND SPIKES! THESE "TERRIBLE LIZARDS" WERE DANGEROUS FROM HEAD TO TOES.

2 DINO-EATING GIANT

This huge 44-ton (40-MT) killing machine roamed North America 150 million years ago. **Allosaurus** sported sawlike teeth that curved backward in its mouth, allowing it to gain a firm grip on its prey: plant-eating dinos.

SOME 40 SPECIES OF DINOSAUR DATING BACK 75 MILLION YEARS HAVE BEEN FOUND IN CANADA'S DINOSAUR PROVINCIAL PARK.

1 TINY AND TERRIBLE

Fierce, fast, and ... the size of a chicken? During the Late Jurassic period, *Compsognathus* was a scary combination for lizards, insects, and other small animals—the prey of this sharp-toothed meat-eater that ran quickly on its back two legs.

⑤ FEARSOME FLOATING PREDATOR

The 50-foot (15-m)-long **Spinosaurus** was the biggest meat-eating dinosaur that ever lived—even bigger than a *Tyrannosaurus rex*. With an enormous six-foot (1.8-m) sail on its back, this dino was adapted to life in the water, where it hunted crocodiles and fish 100 million years ago.

⑧ COMPACT AND CLEVER

Considered one of the most intelligent dinosaurs, the birdlike *Troodon* had a big brain for its small size (about three feet [1 m] tall and eight feet [2.4 m] long). Its relative smarts, well-developed hearing, and large eyes made it a good nocturnal hunter and a danger to its favorite prey: small lizards, mammals, and invertebrates.

④ HEAD-BUTTING HERBIVORE

Late Cretaceous-era **Pachycephalosaurus** used its domed, bony noggin to whack other dinos. This hard helmet—already an intimidating attribute at up to nine inches (23 cm) thick—actually grew with age!

⑦ POWERFUL PREDATOR

With 50 teeth that were as sharp as knives, as long as bananas, and strong enough to crush bone, *Tyrannosaurus rex* was one bad beast. Its skull alone was five feet (1.5 m) long! This colossal, carnivorous, Late Cretaceous creature could be twice as heavy as an African elephant, the largest living land animal on Earth.

> DINOSAUR REMAINS HAVE BEEN FOUND ON EVERY CONTINENT IN THE WORLD, INCLUDING ANTARCTICA.

③ SLASH AND GNASH

With a name that means "terrible claw," **Deinonychus** was a fast-moving Cretaceous-era carnivore that used the long, curving claws on its feet to slash its unfortunate victims and its 70 jagged teeth to tear them apart.

⑥ SCARY TAILS

Stegosaurus moved slowly but carried a big club. At the end of the two rows of tall plates that ran down its back was a spiked tail, which the 30-foot (9-m)-long Late Jurassic plant-eater could swing at the pesky predators who threatened it.

49

1

LEGGY LUNCH
Chew thoroughly! That wiggly *sannakji*—a Korean dish consisting of **raw octopus**—might still be moving its limbs on the way down.

EIGHT
FEARLESS FOODS
FEELING HUNGRY? PEOPLE ACROSS THE GLOBE DEEM THESE DISHES DOWNRIGHT DELICIOUS.

THE JAPANESE DISH OF PUFFER FISH CAN BE DEADLY TO DINERS IF ITS TOXIC PARTS ARE NOT REMOVED PROPERLY.

2

EIGHT-LEGGED SNACK
While in Cambodia, enjoy *a-ping*, **fried tarantulas** seasoned with salt and sugar. The legs may be crunchy, but beware: The abdomen can be a little gooey.

4 BEWITCHING BITE

Witchetty grubs are **large moth larvae** found in the Australian outback that are traditionally eaten alive and raw. Rich in protein, they have been a staple of the Aboriginal diet.

3 ESCAMOLES

These egg-shaped entities with the consistency of cottage cheese are "insect caviar"—**ant larvae**, used in Mexican dishes since the time of the Aztec.

5 WRIGGLY FARE

On the Pacific island of Samoa, *palolo worms* are scooped up from the sea and enjoyed raw, fried with butter, or even spread on toast.

PEOPLE DRINK COFFEE BREWED FROM BEANS EATEN AND POOPED OUT BY ANIMALS.

7 CHEESE AND CRITTERS

Casu marzu is a traditional Sardinian cheese that contains **live—yes, *live!*—maggots.** They can jump around when disturbed by cutting or spreading and actually survive even after being swallowed.

6 HUNGRY FOR HAGGIS?

This national dish of Scotland is a pudding of **sheep's liver, lungs, and heart** mixed with onion, oatmeal, and spices—stuffed into a sheep's stomach and boiled.

8 ALL EYES ON YOU

Your dinner is staring! While in Japan you can dine on **giant, fatty tuna eyeballs**—including the connective tissue from around the peepers.

51

SPECTACULAR **SPACE** SIGHTS

THESE GALACTICALLY COOL COSMIC SHOTS ARE UNIVERSALLY OUT-OF-THIS-WORLD.

2 GALACTIC HAT

Named for its resemblance to the Mexican hat of the same name, the **Sombrero galaxy** features a glowing, bulging core of stars enclosed in thick, dark lanes of dust.

1 SUPERSTELLAR

Ancient Chinese and Japanese astronomers witnessed the supernova explosion that created the **Crab Nebula** in A.D. 1054. This detailed mosaic image of the six-light-year-wide dead star is the work of NASA's Hubble Space Telescope.

3 FLYING FREE

It's just what it looks like! Mission Specialist Bruce McCandless II performed an **untethered space walk,** going farther unattached to his shuttle than any astronaut had before.

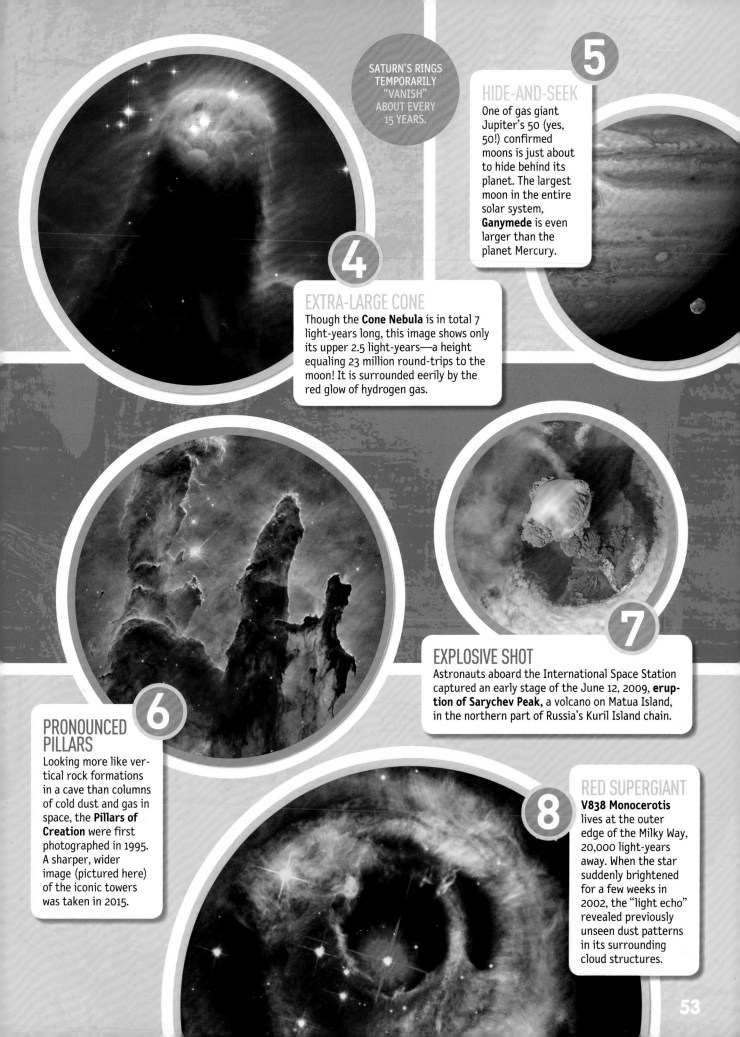

SATURN'S RINGS TEMPORARILY "VANISH" ABOUT EVERY 15 YEARS.

5

HIDE-AND-SEEK

One of gas giant Jupiter's 50 (yes, 50!) confirmed moons is just about to hide behind its planet. The largest moon in the entire solar system, **Ganymede** is even larger than the planet Mercury.

4

EXTRA-LARGE CONE

Though the **Cone Nebula** is in total 7 light-years long, this image shows only its upper 2.5 light-years—a height equaling 23 million round-trips to the moon! It is surrounded eerily by the red glow of hydrogen gas.

6

PRONOUNCED PILLARS

Looking more like vertical rock formations in a cave than columns of cold dust and gas in space, the **Pillars of Creation** were first photographed in 1995. A sharper, wider image (pictured here) of the iconic towers was taken in 2015.

7

EXPLOSIVE SHOT

Astronauts aboard the International Space Station captured an early stage of the June 12, 2009, **eruption of Sarychev Peak**, a volcano on Matua Island, in the northern part of Russia's Kuril Island chain.

8

RED SUPERGIANT

V838 Monocerotis lives at the outer edge of the Milky Way, 20,000 light-years away. When the star suddenly brightened for a few weeks in 2002, the "light echo" revealed previously unseen dust patterns in its surrounding cloud structures.

1
MAGNET FOR SPEED
The force from powerful magnets causes China's **Maglev bullet train** to hover about four inches (10 cm) in the air, pushing it forward at superspeeds. The latest models of this levitating locomotive can cover a mile (1.6 km) in about ten seconds.

THE WORLD'S LONGEST TRAIN— USED JUST ONCE TO HAUL IRON ORE IN AUSTRALIA—WAS AS LONG AS 13 FREEDOM TOWERS LAID END TO END.

EIGHT
TOTALLY COOL TRAINS

ALL ABOARD! WHEN IT COMES TO STYLE AND SPEED, THESE TRAINS ARE OFF-THE-RAILS RAD. FROM SLEEK SUBWAYS TO EYE-POPPING PASSENGER CARS, YOU'LL BE LOCO FOR THESE LOCOMOTIVES.

2
FEELING BLUE
From the *Blue Train,* you get an unbeatable view of South Africa's savanna. In the 24-hour trip from Pretoria to Cape Town, guests are lavished with butler service, gourmet dinners, and glimpses of wildlife like zebras and giraffes grazing in the grassland.

GOING GREEN

The **Inspiro System** commuter trains in Warsaw, Poland, are said to be made of nearly 98 percent recyclable material. Inside, you can hang on to tree-shaped poles, a nod to the train's eco-friendly vibe.

ROYAL RAILS

Get a taste of royalty on the rails while riding this commuter train on Paris, France's subway, which has decor dedicated to the **Palace of Versailles**. Golden sculptures and intricate paintings on the ceilings are just some of the artistic elements on this train.

DRESSED TO KILT

Talk about an exclusive experience: The *Royal Scotsman* train carries just 36 passengers at a time along Scotland's emerald green coastline. Guests gobble meals prepared by a famous chef and lounge on cushy couches. Just don't forget to pack your kilt!

OUT AND BACK

It takes three days to cross Australia's outback on the **Ghan,** named after the Afghans who first explored the country's "red center" on camels over a hundred years ago. Take a close look out the window and you'll spy Uluru, one the world's largest rock formations.

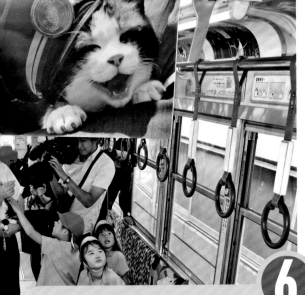

KITTY TRAIN

For years Tama the cat welcomed passengers to Kishi Station in Kinokawa, Japan. She passed away at the age of 16, but her legacy purrs on in a **cat-themed train** covered with cartoon images of the kitty and even whiskers painted on the front.

TRAIN CHIC

Ooh la la! A French fashion designer put his own twist on the design of this **high-speed train** in Paris, France, including plush purple and green seats and colorful countertops in the café car. Sure puts a new spin on traveling in style!

EIGHT ROBOTS THAT ROCK

NEED TO STASH YOUR LUGGAGE OR FIND A BOOK IN THE LIBRARY? THERE'S A ROBOT FOR THAT. YOU WON'T BELIEVE WHAT THESE MIND-BLOWING 'BOTS CAN DO.

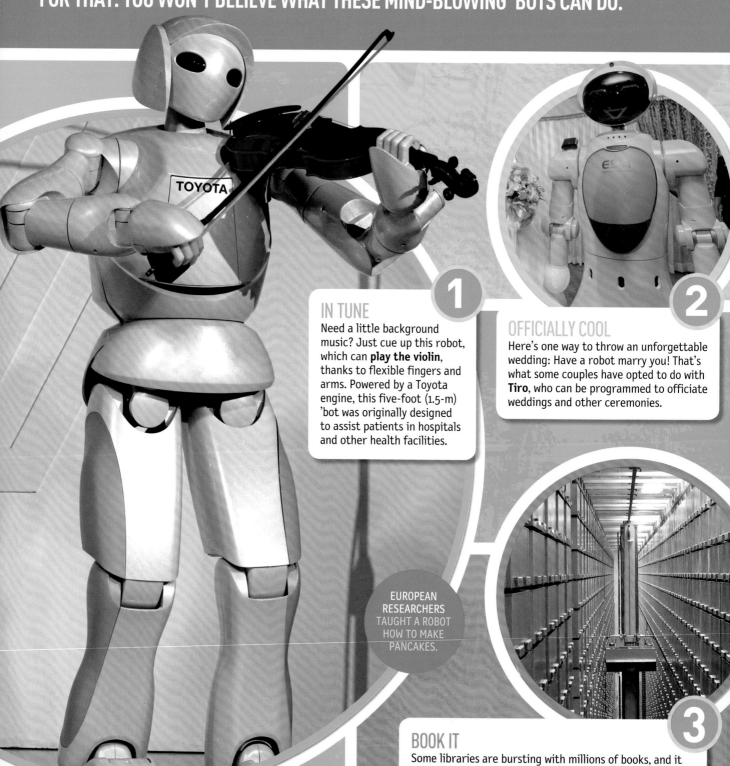

1 IN TUNE
Need a little background music? Just cue up this robot, which can **play the violin**, thanks to flexible fingers and arms. Powered by a Toyota engine, this five-foot (1.5-m) 'bot was originally designed to assist patients in hospitals and other health facilities.

2 OFFICIALLY COOL
Here's one way to throw an unforgettable wedding: Have a robot marry you! That's what some couples have opted to do with **Tiro**, who can be programmed to officiate weddings and other ceremonies.

EUROPEAN RESEARCHERS TAUGHT A ROBOT HOW TO MAKE PANCAKES.

3 BOOK IT
Some libraries are bursting with millions of books, and it can be hard to track down the one you're looking for. But with the touch of a few buttons, the **BookBot** automatically retrieves it for you. Now you have more time to read!

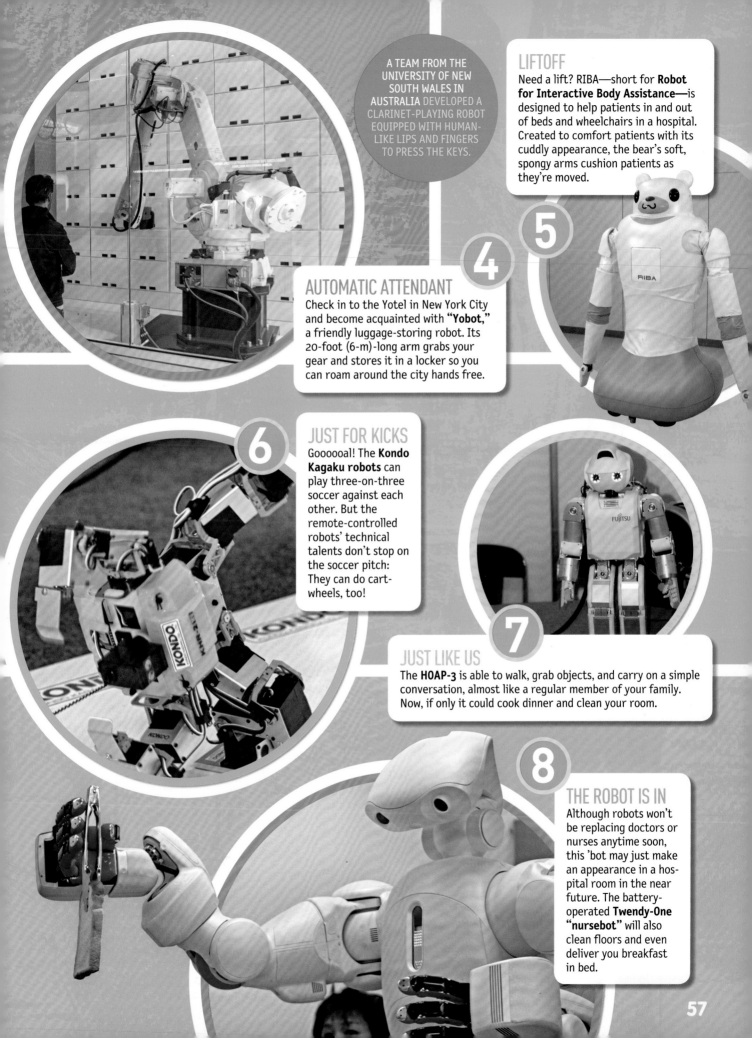

LIFTOFF

5

Need a lift? RIBA—short for **Robot for Interactive Body Assistance**—is designed to help patients in and out of beds and wheelchairs in a hospital. Created to comfort patients with its cuddly appearance, the bear's soft, spongy arms cushion patients as they're moved.

AUTOMATIC ATTENDANT

4

Check in to the Yotel in New York City and become acquainted with **"Yobot,"** a friendly luggage-storing robot. Its 20-foot (6-m)-long arm grabs your gear and stores it in a locker so you can roam around the city hands free.

JUST FOR KICKS

6

Goooooal! The **Kondo Kagaku robots** can play three-on-three soccer against each other. But the remote-controlled robots' technical talents don't stop on the soccer pitch: They can do cart-wheels, too!

JUST LIKE US

7

The **HOAP-3** is able to walk, grab objects, and carry on a simple conversation, almost like a regular member of your family. Now, if only it could cook dinner and clean your room.

THE ROBOT IS IN

8

Although robots won't be replacing doctors or nurses anytime soon, this 'bot may just make an appearance in a hospital room in the near future. The battery-operated **Twendy-One "nursebot"** will also clean floors and even deliver you breakfast in bed.

FANTASTIC FORMATIONS

1

Deep underground in the Shenandoah Valley of Virginia, U.S.A., sprawling **Luray Caverns** is filled with rock formations called stalactites (hanging from the ceiling) and stalagmites (rising from the floor). All the formations—some ten stories high—are calcite, a form of limestone.

THE FORMATIONS **IN LURAY CAVERNS** GROW 1 CUBIC INCH (16.4 CUBIC CM) EVERY 120 YEARS.

WEIRD WONDERS

COLORFUL, CAVERNOUS, OR JUST PLAIN CURIOUS: FEAST YOUR EYES ON SOME OF NATURE'S UNCANNIEST ATTRACTIONS.

AMAZING CRATER

2

Algae, sulfur, salt, and other minerals help create this brightly colored crater of the **Dallol volcano**—Earth's lowest land volcano—located in the Danakil Depression in the northern part of Ethiopia.

RAINBOW RIVER

3

The water level and the amount of sunlight reaching *Macarenia clavigera*, a plant living on this river floor in Colombia, have to be just right. For a few months a year, **Caño Cristales** ("river of five colors") turns bright red—and, in some places, hot pink, bright green, blue, yellow, and orange—making a liquid rainbow.

MIGHTY WATERFALL

4

On the border of Zambia and Zimbabwe, **Victoria Falls** is the largest curtain of water in the world. Spanning a width of 5,600 feet (1,707 m), it's more than twice as wide as the height of the tallest building in the world (see page 103).

THINK PINK!

5

No one knows exactly why this 1,970-foot (600-m)-long lake in Western Australia is the color of bubble gum. Scientists speculate that **Lake Hillier's** color—which stays pink even when the water is bottled—comes from algae, bacteria, or salt.

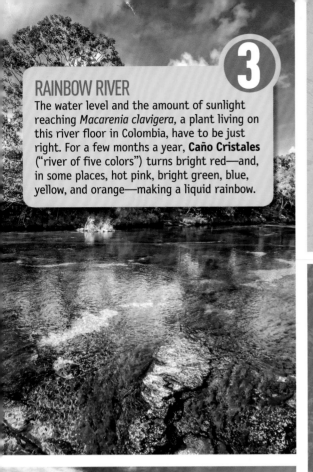

ALL CRACKED UP

6

These rows of brown rectangles at **Eaglehawk Neck** in Tasmania, Australia, look like they were hand-carved out of mud. But this "tessellated pavement" is a geological formation caused by pressure at the Earth's crust that made perpendicular cracks in the rock millions of years ago.

HUMONGOUS HOLE

7

The massive 570-foot (174-m)-deep **Barringer Crater** in the desert of Arizona, U.S.A., was caused by a meteorite slamming into Earth some 50,000 years ago. The 150,000-ton (136,078-MT) space rock hit the ground at a speed of 7.4 miles per second (12 km/sec)—15 times faster than the average bullet.

SALT OF THE EARTH

8

Spreading for thousands of square miles in remote southwestern Bolivia is **Salar de Uyuni**—the world's largest salt flat (dried-up lake), also home to the Luna Salada hotel. Almost everything in the hotel—including the floors, walls, tables, and chairs—is made of salt.

Wet & Wild

READY TO TAKE THE PLUNGE? WHETHER YOU'RE UP FOR A SUPER-STEEP DROP OR A LOOPY LUGE, THESE STOMACH-FLIPPING WATERSLIDES ARE SERIOUSLY SICK. HANG ON TIGHT!

WATERSLIDES

IN NORTH AMERICA ALONE, SOME 82 MILLION PEOPLE VISIT WATER PARKS EVERY YEAR.

①

WHAT: Leap of Faith
WHERE: Dubai, United Arab Emirates
WHY IT'S WICKED: Climb to the top of a Maya temple replica, then drop 60 feet (18.3 m) before shooting through a clear tunnel in a lagoon stocked with sharks.

HOME TO MORE THAN 200 WATERSLIDES, WISCONSIN DELLS IS KNOWN AS THE "WATER PARK CAPITAL OF THE WORLD."

WHAT: Mammoth Indiana
WHERE: Santa Claus, Indiana, U.S.A.
WHY IT'S WICKED: A seven-story drop covering the length of three football fields makes this one of the world's longest waterslides. But you don't have to go it alone: The ride's rafts fit up to six people.

WHAT: Tsunami Surge
WHERE: Austell, Georgia, U.S.A.
WHY IT'S WICKED: It's the world's first zero-gravity waterslide, so you'll feel completely weightless for a couple of seconds when you hit a 40-foot (12-m)-high wave wall.

WHAT: Magic Eye
WHERE: Erding, Germany
WHY IT'S WICKED: Totally tubular! You'll get tunnel vision riding inside this slide, which, at nearly 1,170 feet (357 m), is the longest inner tube waterslide on the planet.

WHAT: Summit Plummet
WHERE: Orlando, Florida, U.S.A.
WHY IT'S WICKED: This 12-story vertical drop has you shooting through an unlit tunnel at a rate of some 60 miles an hour (97 km/h). Hope you're not afraid of the dark!

WHAT: Verrückt
WHERE: Kansas City, Kansas, U.S.A.
WHY IT'S WICKED: Verrückt means "insane" in German, and this slide is just that. The world's tallest *and* fastest waterslide, Verrückt features a drop from a height taller than Niagara Falls and has riders reaching top speeds of around 65 miles an hour (105 km/h).

WHAT: The Wedgie
WHERE: Gold Coast, Queensland, Australia
WHY IT'S WICKED: Brave this slide and you'll fall at a rate of 38 feet per second (11.7 m/s) as you're sent along stomach-flipping 360-degree loops—which, yes, may lead to the unfortunate bathing suit wedgie once you reach the end. We warned you!

WHAT: Insano
WHERE: Aquiraz, Brazil
WHY IT'S WICKED: This ride is short and steep: It takes just five terrifying seconds to reach the bottom of this nearly vertical drop from 14 stories above.

TURN THE PAGE FOR MORE!

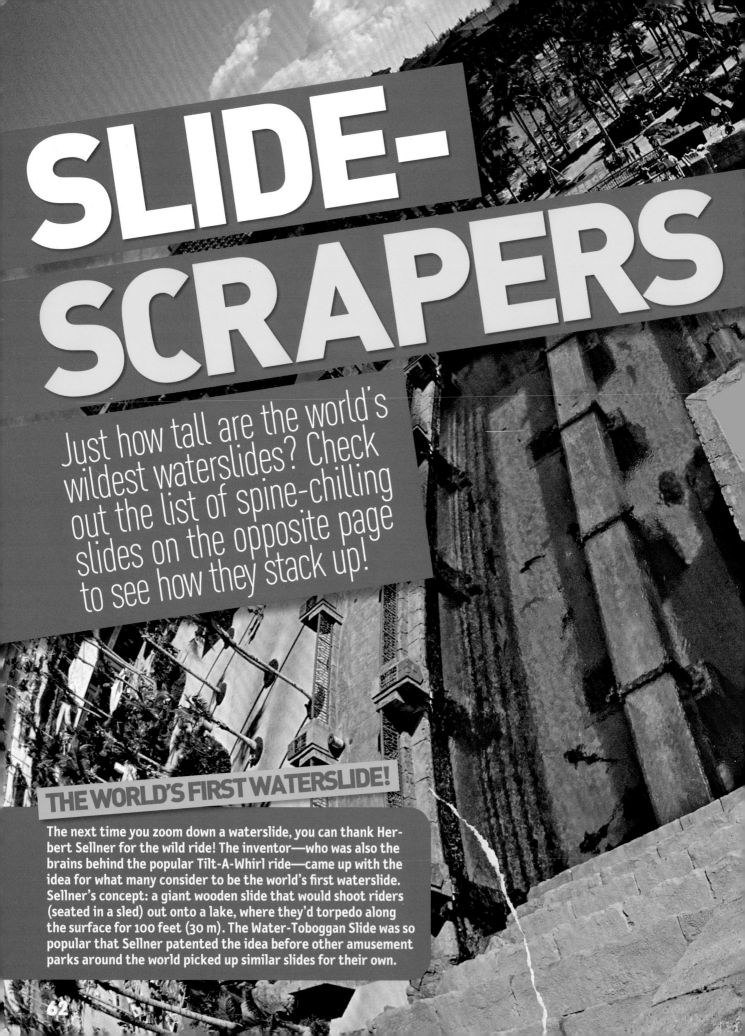

SLIDE-SCRAPERS

Just how tall are the world's wildest waterslides? Check out the list of spine-chilling slides on the opposite page to see how they stack up!

THE WORLD'S FIRST WATERSLIDE!

The next time you zoom down a waterslide, you can thank Herbert Sellner for the wild ride! The inventor—who was also the brains behind the popular Tilt-A-Whirl ride—came up with the idea for what many consider to be the world's first waterslide. Sellner's concept: a giant wooden slide that would shoot riders (seated in a sled) out onto a lake, where they'd torpedo along the surface for 100 feet (30 m). The Water-Toboggan Slide was so popular that Sellner patented the idea before other amusement parks around the world picked up similar slides for their own.

GET READY FOR A NEAR-VERTICAL LEAP OF FAITH!

BRACE YOURSELF FOR VERRÜCKT!

RIDERS PLUMMET 65 MILES AN HOUR (105 KM/H) ON INSANO.

WATERSLIDE: Verrückt
LOCATION: Kansas City, Kansas, U.S.A.
HEIGHT: 168 feet 7 inches (51 m)

WATERSLIDE: Kilimanjaro
LOCATION: Barra do Piraí, Brazil
HEIGHT: 164 feet (49 m)

WATERSLIDE: Captain Spacemaker
LOCATION: Venice, Italy
HEIGHT: 138 feet (42 m)

WATERSLIDE: Insano
LOCATION: Aquiraz, Brazil
HEIGHT: 135 feet (41 m)

WATERSLIDE: Deep Water Dive
LOCATION: Louisville, Kentucky, U.S.A.
HEIGHT: 121 feet (37 m)

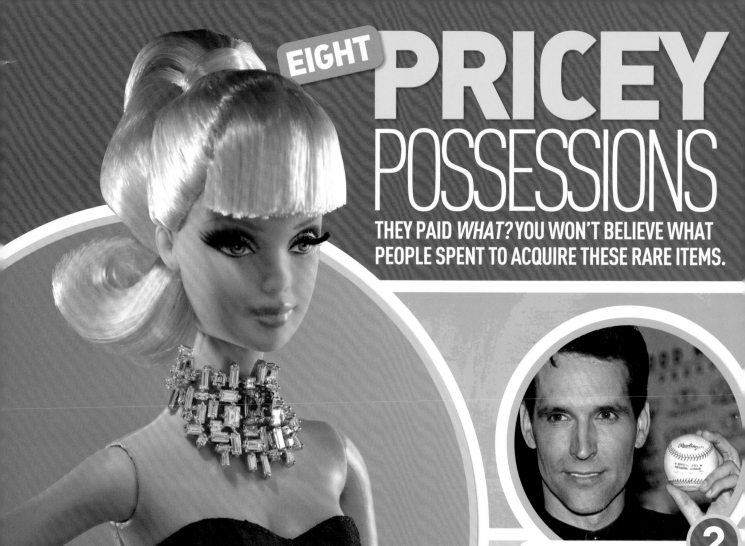

PRICEY POSSESSIONS

THEY PAID *WHAT?* YOU WON'T BELIEVE WHAT PEOPLE SPENT TO ACQUIRE THESE RARE ITEMS.

2

RECORD-BREAKING BALL
Comic book creator Todd McFarlane (pictured) paid **$3 million** for the ball major league baseball player Mark McGwire hit for his record-breaking 70th home run of the 1998 season.

1

BLINGED-OUT BARBIE
Australian jewelry designer Stefano Canturi designed this special-edition one-of-a-kind doll, which was sold at auction for **$302,500**—making it the most expensive Barbie ever sold. (Those are real diamonds she's wearing!)

3

HIGH-PRICED HAIR
Singer Elvis Presley was famous not only for his music but also for his mane. A small jar containing some of the late entertainer's hair once sold for **$115,000**.

4

PRETTY IN PINK
British jeweler and billionaire Laurence Graff bought this 24.78-carat rare pink diamond for more than **$45 million** in 2010—spending the most anyone had ever paid for a jewel.

5

SUPERMAN, SUPERPRICE
A well-preserved copy of Action Comics No. 1, the 1938 comic featuring the first appearance of the Man of Steel, sold for **$3,207,852** in a 2014 online auction.

6

RARE RACER
Car enthusiasts eager to own one of these rare, mid-20th-century racers have spent millions for a speedy piece of history. A private buyer in the United Kingdom reportedly paid nearly **$40 million** for a 1957 Ferrari 250 Testa Rossa.

7

FABULOUS FEATHER
The most expensive feather ever sold, this single quill was purchased at auction for $8,000 New Zealand dollars (at the time about U.S. **$5,500**). It's a feather from the huia bird, which has not been spotted since 1907 and is thought to be extinct.

ONE COMPANY OFFERS A LIMITED-EDITION 24-KARAT-GOLD EXTREME MOUNTAIN BIKE FEATURING MORE THAN 600 BLACK DIAMONDS AND 500 GOLDEN SAPPHIRES.

8

LUKE'S LIGHTSABER
A not-so-long time ago at an auction house not too far away, a serious *Star Wars* fan paid **$240,000** to own the lightsaber Luke Skywalker used in the first two movies of the original cinematic trilogy. (The force was strong with that one.)

EIGHT

Works of Mind-Bending STREET ART

YOUR EYES DON'T DECEIVE YOU! THESE OPEN-AIR WORKS OF ART WILL MAKE YOU STOP IN YOUR TRACKS.

2

ABOUT FACE

Toronto, Canada–based visual artist Dan Bergeron created this amazing illusion as part of his **"Face of the City"** series, which incorporates the surfaces of urban walls into his works of art.

KOLAMS ARE COLORFUL FLOOR DRAWINGS MADE FROM RICE FLOUR.

1

RUNAWAY RAILCAR

This 3-D painting depicting a soon-to-be precarious predicament was part of a "Magic Art" special exhibition in the city of Hangzhou, China.

5 HOLE-Y MOLEY!

Whoa—that's a bad one. Actually, it's a really great illusion by artists 3D Joe and Max displayed in Trafalgar Square, London, England, calling attention to the **pitfalls of potholes.**

8 NOAH'S ARK

This sprawling three-dimensional reimagining of the **flood tale** was painted on Valois Square in Wilhelmshaven, Germany.

4 WHERE'S WALDO?

French street artist Oakoak's illusion references the children's book series that challenges readers to find the **hidden main character** among large groups of people in different locations.

7 DIVE IN!

Artists 3D Joe and Max created this work to commemorate the two-year anniversary of the **London 2012 Olympics.** It features iconic scenery as well as athletes from the games.

3 HANGING AROUND

Created outside the main entrance to the Corinthia Hotel in London, England, this incredible 3-D depiction features the likeness of a **crystal chandelier** in the hotel's Lobby Lounge.

6 LONG JUMP

Can you make it **across the abyss?** This amazing 3-D scene is painted on the dam on Dunajec River in Niedzica, Poland.

EIGHT

WACKY WAYS TO GET THERE

CHECK OUT THESE UNCONVENTIONAL MODES OF TRANSPORTATION TO NAVIGATE YOUR WAY ON LAND, BY SEA, AND BEYOND.

1

BIKE LIKE
With no pedals, no seat, and no gears, **FLIZ** harnesses the rider between the wheels and relies on his or her foot power to keep the bike running.

2

REINDEER SLEDGE
It's not just for Santa anymore! Visitors to the province of Lapland, Finland—which has roughly the same number of reindeer as people—can enjoy **sleigh rides** just like St. Nick.

4

GIDDYUP!
Hundreds of thousands of adventurous visitors to the Grand Canyon, in Arizona, U.S.A., have been taking **mule rides** down into its inner depths since the 1800s. Visitors who prefer to stay higher up can ride around the canyon's rim.

3

SUPERCHARGED SUBMERSIBLE
This submersible watercraft with a super-charged engine can jump 90 degrees out of the water. Two passengers can fit inside the 17-foot (5.2-m)-long, 3-foot (1-m)-wide shark-style **Seabreacher X,** which even has an upholstered interior and a sound system.

5

CYCLE RICKSHAW
Also known as velotaxis, bike taxis, and more, **pedicabs** are for-hire urban transportation powered by humans ped-aling—instead of pulling, as in a traditional rickshaw.

6

TICKET, PLEASE!
Ready to soar above Earth's atmosphere as a **space tourist?** In recent years private compa-nies such as billionaire Sir Richard Branson's Virgin Galactic have begun to work toward making space travel a reality for nonastronauts.

7

PERSONAL FLIGHT MACHINE
The **Martin Jetpack** has been shown in testing to reach a speed of up to 46 miles an hour (74 km/h) and an altitude of up to 3,280 feet (1,000 m) for more than 30 minutes.

MONSTER SCHOOL BUS
How would you like to roll up to school in this awesome yellow machine? **"Higher Education"** is a vehicle in the fleet of Vaters Motorsports, a professional monster-truck race team based in Maryland, U.S.A.

8

EIGHT WICKED WEAPONS
IN HISTORY
LETHAL INVENTIONS! FOR THOUSANDS OF YEARS WARRIORS HAVE WIELDED SOME SPINE-CHILLING TOOLS OF DESTRUCTION.

2 SEEING STARS
Commonly known as "throwing stars," **shuriken** are thousand-year-old traditional Japanese weapons that could be concealed in the hands of ninjas and launched in surprise attacks against opponents.

1 PETRIFYING POLEARM
Dating back more than a thousand years to China, a **guan dao** could be used to make sweeping slashes at unwanted aggressors. Used today in some forms of martial arts, this intimidating implement also features a notch on the blade that can be used for catching an enemy's weapon.

3 RAMMING SPEED!
You're going to need to bring in some friends for this one! A **battering ram** was basically a log shoved with great force against a fortification in the hope of cracking and ultimately breaking through. It required some serious manpower to operate.

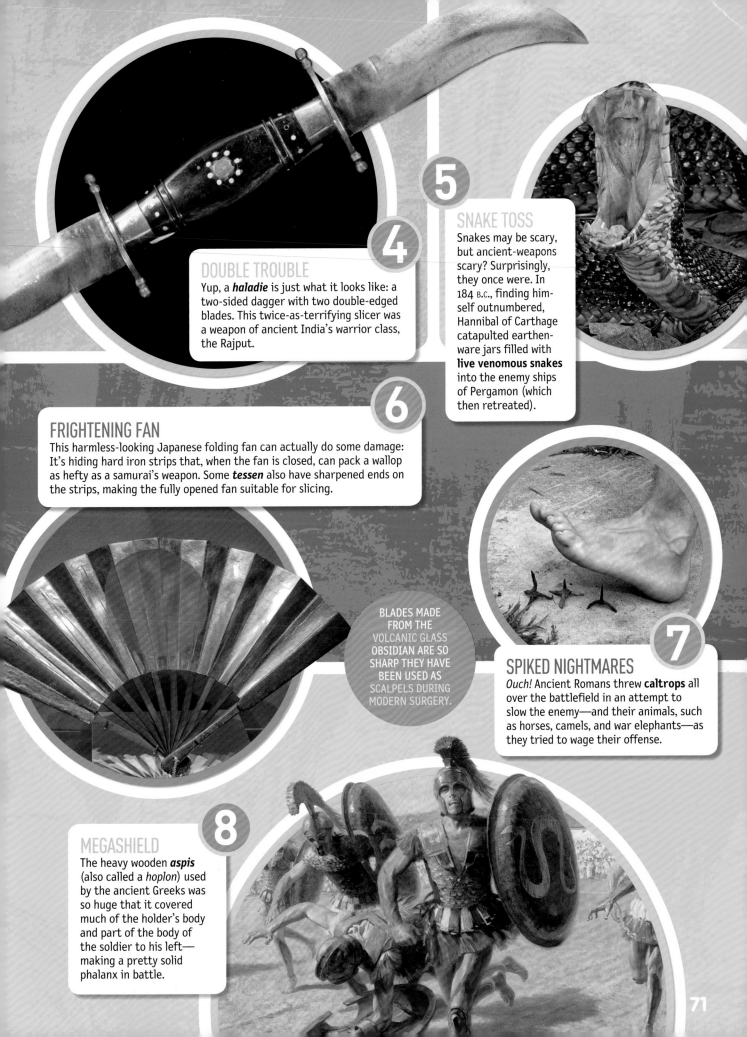

4 DOUBLE TROUBLE

Yup, a **haladie** is just what it looks like: a two-sided dagger with two double-edged blades. This twice-as-terrifying slicer was a weapon of ancient India's warrior class, the Rajput.

5 SNAKE TOSS

Snakes may be scary, but ancient-weapons scary? Surprisingly, they once were. In 184 B.C., finding himself outnumbered, Hannibal of Carthage catapulted earthenware jars filled with **live venomous snakes** into the enemy ships of Pergamon (which then retreated).

6 FRIGHTENING FAN

This harmless-looking Japanese folding fan can actually do some damage: It's hiding hard iron strips that, when the fan is closed, can pack a wallop as hefty as a samurai's weapon. Some **tessen** also have sharpened ends on the strips, making the fully opened fan suitable for slicing.

BLADES MADE FROM THE VOLCANIC GLASS OBSIDIAN ARE SO SHARP THEY HAVE BEEN USED AS SCALPELS DURING MODERN SURGERY.

7 SPIKED NIGHTMARES

Ouch! Ancient Romans threw **caltrops** all over the battlefield in an attempt to slow the enemy—and their animals, such as horses, camels, and war elephants—as they tried to wage their offense.

8 MEGASHIELD

The heavy wooden *aspis* (also called a *hoplon*) used by the ancient Greeks was so huge that it covered much of the holder's body and part of the body of the soldier to his left—making a pretty solid phalanx in battle.

1

RUNS ON RAYS

Forget gas: This car is powered by the sun! The roof of the **PowerCore SunCruiser** is covered with solar cells, which soak up rays that charge its electric engine.

CRAZIEST CARS

A SEDAN SHAPED LIKE A SHARK. A CAR POWERED BY THE SUN. YOU'LL WANT TO GET BEHIND THE WHEEL OF THESE OUTRAGEOUS VEHICLES. BUCKLE UP!

A BLINGED-OUT MERCEDES-BENZ DECORATED WITH MORE THAN ONE MILLION CRYSTALS SOLD AT AUCTION FOR NEARLY $240,000.

2

SHARK ON LAND

This shark-shaped art car named **Ripper** brings the fearsome fish to the roads. But don't worry: Despite the jaw full of terrifying teeth, Ripper is totally friendly.

4 IN CONTROL

No driver's license? No problem! The Mercedes-Benz **self-driving car**, still in concept form, doesn't require a driver behind the wheel. Simply plug in your destination and a robot controls the steering and the speed. All you have to do is pick what to play on the radio!

3 SUPERHERO STATUS

To the Batcave! This sleek sports car is an exact replica of the **Batmobile** featured in the Batman movies. It can zip along the streets as fast as 180 miles an hour (290 km/h) thanks to a powerful engine previously used in a military helicopter.

5 CUSTOM CAR

The handcrafted **Tramontana R** race car is designed to match the specific requests of its driver, including color and material. The custom car is also superspeedy, able to go from 0 to 60 miles an hour (97 km/h) in just four seconds.

6 ROCK-AND-ROLL

What a scream! This **1970 Volkswagen Beetle** has been transformed to look like a rock band's lead singer, including his face, hair, and trademark tongue. Just imagine the looks you'd get if you hit the streets in this!

7 SEEING DOUBLE

These **stacked VW Beetles** are just some of the creative concepts you'll see at the annual Art Car Parade in Houston, Texas, U.S.A. The 30-year-old event attracts hundreds of artists showing off their souped-up, funky cars to vie for a $15,000 prize.

BEST FOOT FORWARD

For years, this iconic **"toe" truck** has welcomed customers outside of a Seattle, Washington, U.S.A., towing company. The pink truck—which can tow a small vehicle—has no doors and stands over 11 feet (3.3 m) tall from wheel to, uh, toenail.

BODACIOUS
Buried TREASURES

WHAT PRECIOUS OBJECTS AND WONDERS LAY BENEATH LAND AND SEA? CHECK OUT THESE INCREDIBLE EXCAVATIONS.

(1)

REMARKABLE RECOVERY

First discovered more than a century ago by sponge divers near the Greek island of **Antikythera**, the wreck—dating to about 60 B.C.—has yielded many artifacts including jewelry, glassware, statues, and an ancient analog computer. Pictured here are a bronze spear that would have belonged to a warrior statue and the upper part of a marble statue of Hermes (inset).

INCREDIBLE WRECK

2

This jewel-encrusted gold belt was recovered from the 1622 wreck of a Spanish ship that sank off the coast of what is now Florida, U.S.A. Part of a fleet of vessels that met the same end, the **Atocha** was carrying tobacco, gems, jewels, copper ingots, silver bullion, gold bars and discs, and more.

AMAZING ARTIFACT

An ancient tomb dating back to the Zhou dynasty (1046–256 B.C.) was discovered during the construction of a hospital in China's Henan Province. This **bronze wine vessel** was among the incredible finds.

4

3

JAW-DROPPING DISCOVERY

More than a hundred silver and gold artifacts dating back a thousand years were discovered … by a retired businessman with a metal detector! Among the **Viking treasures** uncovered in a southwest Scotland field were an early Christian cross, armbands, and brooches like the golden pin pictured here.

5

SHOCKING STOCKPILE

A collection of **108 gold coins** was found under a floor tile in an ancient castle north of Tel Aviv, Israel, the site of Crusades-era battles between Christian and Muslim forces. Researchers believe that the treasure was hidden to keep it from invading conquerors in the mid-13th century.

6

MIND-BLOWING FIND

Nearly **2,000 gold coins** were discovered off the coast of the ancient city of Caesarea, Israel, by amateur scuba divers. Members of the diving club at first thought the thousand-year-old coins were toys!

7

STUNNING STASH

Pieces of **gold and silver jewelry** dating back 2,000 years were discovered during the renovation of a department store about 50 miles (80 km) northeast of London, England. Archaeologists believe a wealthy Roman woman stashed her treasure for safekeeping during a British tribe's bloody revolt against Roman rule in 61 A.D.

8

AWE-INSPIRING ALEXANDRIA

Talk about face-to-face with history! This **black granite sphinx**—believed to have represented Ptolemy XII, father of Cleopatra—was one of many ancient treasures uncovered during excavations in the harbor of Alexandria, Egypt.

TURN THE PAGE TO FIND OUT MORE!

REVEALED: UNDERWATER ALEXANDRIA

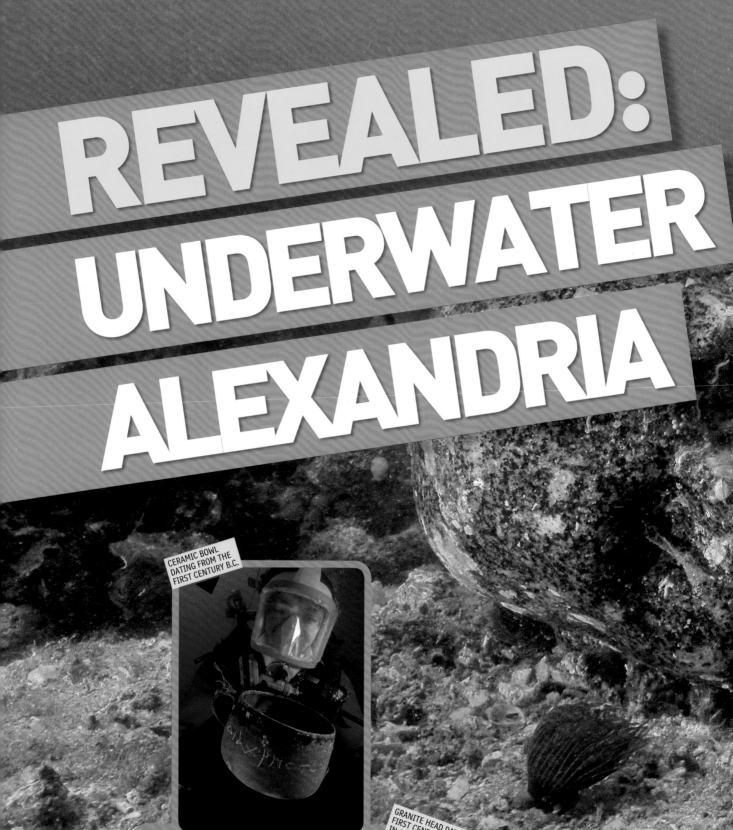

CERAMIC BOWL DATING FROM THE FIRST CENTURY B.C.

GRANITE HEAD DATING FROM THE FIRST CENTURY B.C., DISCOVERED IN ALEXANDRIA'S HARBOR

Alexandria was founded in 331 B.C. by Alexander the Great, legendary Macedonian military commander and empire builder. A beacon of science, culture, and scholarship, the ancient coastal metropolis along the Mediterranean Sea was known for its Great Library (at one time the largest in the world) and for its towering Pharos lighthouse, one of the Seven Wonders of the Ancient World. But over time multiple severe earthquakes rocked the ancient port city and sent significant parts of it into the sea. Palaces, temples, and other structures sank to the harbor floor where they sat for centuries under sand and sediment.

In the 1990s scientists began mapping the scarcely explored harbor floor and have since located and cataloged an astonishing range of underwater artifacts—including colossal statues, columns, obelisks, sphinxes, ceramics, coins, and jewelry—from this influential ancient city. Among the finds have been thousands of huge stone blocks, including some from the Pharos lighthouse, which is thought to have collapsed into the water in the wake of the earthquakes.

Another incredible revelation brought to light through a combination of diving and advanced technology is that the basic structures of temples, military posts, and royal palaces remained intact. Punishing earthquakes in the fourth and eighth centuries A.D., along with tsunamis and a gradual sinking, had caused the edge of the magnificent city to slide into the sea. Among the amazing finds were the ruins of a palace and temple complex of one of Alexandria's most famous residents: Cleopatra.

THONIS-HERACLEION: LEGENDARY EXCAVATION

BURIED UNDER THE SEA for more than 1,200 years, the ancient Egyptian city of Thonis-Heracleion was rediscovered in 2000 by French archaeologist Franck Goddio, who was deliberately searching for the mysterious city that was mentioned in ancient texts. For years Goddio undertook the mammoth task of locating Thonis-Heracleion in a survey area of more than 27,000 acres (11,000 ha). Known as Heracleion to the ancient Greeks and Thonis to the ancient Egyptians, the city—likely founded around the eighth century B.C.—disappeared into the waters of the Mediterranean in the eighth century A.D. after damage sustained by natural disasters. The site lies east of Alexandria, in Aboukir Bay.

Well preserved and protected by thick layers of sand and mud on the seafloor, the artifacts discovered and unearthed by Goddio and his team have revealed that Heracleion was an important hub of international trade. More than 60 shipwrecks and 700 ancient anchors dating from the sixth to the second centuries B.C. have been found, along with gold coins, weights made from bronze and stone, jewelry, and ceramics. A huge stone slab (a stele) inscribed in both ancient Egyptian and ancient Greek has also been brought to the surface.

Scientists aren't exactly sure why Thonis-Heracleion sunk, but the city's weighty buildings may have become too heavy for the area's post-earthquake waterlogged earth. This, plus a gradual rise in sea level, may have caused the city's ground to collapse beneath it.

COOLEST KINDS
OF CAMOUFLAGE

CAN YOU SPOT THE CONCEALED CRITTERS? THEY MAY BLEND IN, BUT THESE MAJESTIC MASTERS OF DISGUISE WILL KEEP YOU LOOKING.

1 HIDDEN ARACHNID
More than 2,000 species of **crab spider** live all over the world, nearly always colored to match their surroundings. These insect-eaters often walk sideways—like a crab!

2 HARD-TO-FIND FLATFISH
Bothus mancus likes to hang out at the sandy bottoms of coral reefs, feeding on crabs, shrimp, and fish in shallow areas of the Indian and Pacific Oceans.

3 CRAFTY CATERPILLAR
Is it the small branch of a pine tree? A needle-covered stick with eyes? Neither! This **lichen-colored caterpillar** becomes almost invisible in its tropical environment of Sarawak, Borneo.

INVISIBLE OWL

This nocturnal bird hides itself from daytime predators by blending in with tree bark, even moving to and fro to imitate a blowing branch. The **scops owl** swoops down from its perch to munch mostly on insects, earthworms, and spiders.

4

5

CLEVER CANINE

A **gray wolf** is camouflaged within these snowy trees. The largest species of wild dog in the world, these pack-living social canines can reach an intimidating weight of up to 176 pounds (80 kg).

RECENT RESEARCH SUGGESTS THAT ZEBRAS' STRIPES—THOUGHT TO HAVE EVOLVED AS CAMOUFLAGE—INSTEAD HELP THEM FEND OFF THE NIBBLES OF BITING FLIES AND STAY COOL IN SUPER-HOT HABITATS.

7

CONCEALED CRUSTACEAN

One of these things is not like the other! Hidden among these willowy-looking limbs is a **coral shrimp** in the waters of Bali, Indonesia.

TOAD TRIO

6

Which are the leaves and which are the ... *toads?* Yes! Unseen among this leaf litter are **three different toads** of the same species hiding in plain sight in Barro Colorado Island, Panama.

INCREDIBLE APPENDAGES

8

The **leafy sea dragon's** leaflike appendages resemble the seaweed in its Australian shallow coastal water habitat, where it enjoys eating tiny crustaceans and sea lice.

1

WHAT: General Carrera Lake
WHERE: Patagonia, Chile
DREAMY DETAILS: Floating above the lake's turquoise surface are majestic marble tunnels, caverns, and columns carved by 6,200 years of waves.

EIGHT
DREAM DESTINATIONS

IF YOU COULD GO ANYWHERE IN THE WORLD, WHERE WOULD YOU GO? CHANCES ARE YOU'D PICK ONE OF THESE STUNNING SPOTS. TAKE A QUICK TRIP TO THE MOST BEAUTIFUL PLACES ON THE PLANET.

2

WHAT: Victoria Peak
WHERE: Hong Kong
DREAMY DETAILS: From the top of Victoria Peak, you can see forever—or at least most of Hong Kong. The 1,800-foot (549-m)-high peak offers sweeping views of the city's skyline and surrounding islands.

WHAT: Sun and sea
WHERE: Santorini, Greece
DREAMY DETAILS: Known as the most beautiful island in Greece, Santorini is highlighted by white-washed buildings tucked into cliffs made of volcanic rock, all overlooking the sparkling waters of the Aegean Sea.

④

FOR ABOUT $400,000 YOU CAN BUY A PRIVATE CARIBBEAN ISLAND—COMPLETE WITH A TWO-BEDROOM HOME AND A WHITE SANDY BEACH—OFF THE COAST OF PANAMA.

③

WHAT: Baobab Trees
WHERE: Madagascar
DREAMY DETAILS: These towering trees aren't the only things that make Madagascar one of the most amazing places on the planet: The world's fourth largest island, it's home to some 200,000 species of animals and is the only place where lemurs live in the wild.

⑤

WHAT: Northern Lights
WHERE: Tromsø, Norway
DREAMY DETAILS: You have to travel way north to get this unbeatable view of the aurora borealis, a magical natural phenomenon produced by the action of solar wind on the atmosphere at Earth's Poles.

⑦

WHAT: Mergui Archipelago
WHERE: Myanmar
DREAMY DETAILS: Want to get away from it all? Book a trip to this land of 800 islands in the Indian Ocean. Known as the "Lost World" because of its isolated location, only about 2,000 people visit here each year.

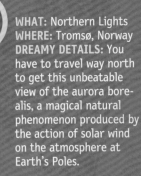

⑥

WHAT: The Dark Hedges
WHERE: Ballymoney, Ireland
DREAMY DETAILS: This mystical tunnel of twisting beech trees leads the way to an Irish mansion. Planted two centuries ago, this arboreal avenue is now one of the most photographed spots in all of Ireland.

⑧

WHAT: Glacier National Park
WHERE: West Glacier, Montana, U.S.A.
DREAMY DETAILS: The main attractions of this park may be the giant glaciers, but its nearly 200 lakes and waterfalls often steal the show. Fed by snowmelt, the lakes in the park are so clear you can spot fish some 30 feet (9 m) below the surface.

EIGHT
INGENIOUS INVENTIONS

FROM A SPEEDY ELECTRIC MOTORCYCLE TO A TRANSPARENT TENT, THESE INNOVATIVE INVENTIONS WILL MAKE YOU WISH FOR THINGS YOU NEVER KNEW EXISTED.

2 PUSH FOR PIZZA
Mama mia! This **fridge magnet** contains a transmitter that places a pizza order with just one touch. It's available only to customers of a pizza place in the United Arab Emirates, but its inventors predict it'll catch on elsewhere.

1 WALL WALKER
Watch out, Spider-Man! This **climbing device** enables its wearer to crawl up walls. How? Two handheld suction pads attached to inexpensive vacuums provide super sticking power, giving mere mortals wall-climbing superpowers.

3 GO WITH THE FLOW
Get a light show every time you wash your hands with this **flashy faucet.** Built-in LED lights within the faucet add a splash of color, with the hues changing according to the water's temperature. Cool!

Much smaller than a motorcycle, the **Uno** is a "dicycle" with two side-by-side wheels that can reach speeds of about 15 miles an hour (24 km/h). Even cooler? It's electric, so it doesn't produce any pollution.

5

4

HAVE A BALL

The **Ping-Pong Door** transforms from a door to a table-tennis court in seconds. Just push the top of the door's built-in panel to unlock it, and then swing it into a horizontal position to get your game on.

6

SO HANDY

An artist invented this **glove** with a built-in microphone and speaker that connects to any standard smart-phone via a wireless Bluetooth signal. Simply slip it on and you can, uh, talk to the hand.

7

STRINGS ATTACHED

This just may be the coolest jungle gym ever. The **String Prototype** is a giant inflatable bubble filled with webs of stretched-out string that's sturdy enough to hold the weight of kids of all ages.

THE CO-INVENTOR OF THE COTTON CANDY MACHINE WAS A DENTIST.

8

BUBBLE TENT

Sleep under the stars without having to worry about being bitten by bugs in the **CristalBubble,** a clear, inflatable tent that has a built-in bed and electricity. Meteor shower, anyone?

Animals in ACTION

FLYING FROGS! DASHING DOGS! THESE CREATURES DEFINITELY PUT THE WILD IN WILDLIFE. CHECK OUT THESE SUPERCOOL SHOTS OF ANIMALS CAUGHT IN THE ACT OF BEING AWESOME!

② WILDE AND FREE

Millions of **wildebeests** make an annual migration through East Africa every May or June. Seeking greener pastures, the migrating mammals will travel nearly 2,000 miles (3,219 km) round-trip.

A GREYHOUND NAMED CINDERELLA ONCE CLEARED A HURDLE MEASURING 68 INCHES (1.7 M), THAT'S TALLER THAN THE AVERAGE TEN-YEAR-OLD.

① WING IT

Boasting a six-foot (1.8-m) wingspan, a **Eurasian eagle-owl** swoops in for the kill. These big birds are not only the largest of all owls, they are also incredibly strong and fast, which makes them powerful hunters.

5
TALL DRINK OF WATER
Because a **giraffe's** neck is actually too short to reach the ground, slurping up water results in a silly, spread-legged split. The bad news? Giraffes are more vulnerable to predators while in this pose. The good news? They need to drink only once every few days.

8
FAST CAT
There's just no catching a **cheetah:** The world's fastest land animal, the spotted cat relies on strong, long legs, a smooth stride, and a streamlined body to reach speeds faster than a car on the highway.

4
LEAP FROG
Experts in the jumping game, **frogs** are the most airborne of all amphibians. How do they do it? Scientists say frogs coil their tendons like springs before launching themselves into the air, allowing them to leap 20 times their own body length in a single bound.

7
GO FISH
When it comes to fishing for its meal, the rare **kingfisher** bird hardly ever misses its mark. The precise hunter typically stalks crustaceans, dragonfly larvae, and fish, gobbling its own body weight in food every day.

3
CLEARING THE AIR
The cat's out of the bag: Some frisky **felines** can jump up to five times their own height in just one leap. The world record—setting human high jumper cleared about one and one-third times his height.

6
DOG-TIRED
A sprint for this **basset hound** is enough to send its tongue wagging. Because of this breed's short legs and droopy ears, it's certainly not the speediest. But being low to the ground makes this breed one of the best sniffers around!

1

NOTHING BUT NET

This playground is made with love! An artistic husband-and-wife team used tons of yarn to braid and crochet these **colorful climbing nets** found in Japan, Singapore, China, and Spain.

A NORWAY PARK'S EQUIPMENT IS MADE ENTIRELY FROM REPURPOSED MATERIALS FROM THE OFFSHORE OIL INDUSTRY, LIKE RIGS AND TANKS.

EIGHT
PLAYGROUNDS THAT BRING THE
FUN!

SWINGS AND SLIDES ARE FUN, BUT WHAT ABOUT CLIMBING AROUND A GIANT TREE HOUSE OR A TILTED TRAIN? YOU CAN TAKE YOUR PLAY TO SOARING NEW LEVELS AT THESE EXTRAORDINARY PARKS AROUND THE WORLD.

2

FULL TILT

Kids go crazy for this tilted train at the **Tiong Bahru Park Adventure Playground** in Singapore. The eccentric park also features a mini-maze and a human-powered merry-go-round.

IT'S A JUNGLE OUT THERE

4

Have a really *wild* time at **Nashville Zoo's Jungle Gym** in Tennessee, U.S.A. Scamper up the 35-foot (10.6-m) Tree of Life tree house, slide through a snake tunnel, or climb aboard a concrete hippo. This park is so big that more than a thousand kids can play here at one time!

TIRED OUT

3

Call it a *tire*-ing effort: Some 3,000 old rubber car and truck tires were repurposed to make swings, tunnels, towering mountains, dragons, and robots at the **Nishi Rokugo Park** in Tokyo, Japan.

UP A HILL

5

A team of designers carved the **Bicentennial Children's Park** out of a steep hillside in Santiago, Chile. Take a cable train to the top of the hill, and then zoom down any of the dozens of slides built into the slope, or stop to take in the view of the city below.

UP ON THE ROOF

7

Head to the top of a convention center in the heart of San Francisco, California, U.S.A., and you'll find the **Yerba Buena Gardens Play Circle**. Splash in play streams, dig around in a sandpit, or shoot down a nearly three-story tube slide. It's an oasis of fun in the bustling big city.

SLINKING AROUND

6

The **City Museum** in St. Louis, Missouri, U.S.A., used to be a shoe warehouse. Today it houses funky collections and features a fun house for all ages, including a sky-high jungle gym and a giant Slinky-like spiral to climb up—all made out of repurposed and recycled materials.

IMAGINATION MOVERS

8

No swings or slides here: At **Imagination Playground** in New York City, the only equipment you'll find are blue foam building blocks in all shapes and sizes. Here, budding architects are encouraged to build structures using the blocks and found items like crates, ropes, and wheels.

EIGHT
Awesome Things in
ANTARCTICA

THERE'S A LOT MORE TO ANTARCTICA THAN ICE, ICE, AND MORE ICE. HERE ARE EIGHT NATURAL WONDERS TO DISCOVER ON THE EARTH'S COLDEST CONTINENT.

① TALL TAIL

Ten species of **whales**, like the humpback seen here, call the continent home. Though some whales may migrate up to 4,000 miles (6,437 km) seeking warmer waters in the winter, the summer months bring them back to the welcoming chill—and the all-you-can-eat krill buffet—that only Antarctica has to offer.

FUR REAL

These **fur seals** are all ears—and eyes! The only eared seal species in Antarctica, these fuzzy mammals are said to resemble large dogs. Their floppy earflaps help them hear oncoming predators, and big eyes help them seek out prey in the dim Arctic waters. As for those fuzzy coats? They're made of thick, waterproof fur that helps the seals stay warm in frigid temps.

2

ABOUT 90 PERCENT OF AN ICEBERG IS BELOW THE WATER'S SURFACE.

COMING UP FOR AIR

Now you see it—now you don't! **Humpback whales** spend most of their time underwater, but you just may spot one breaching above the surface. Experts think the whales leap to shake off pesky skin parasites—or maybe just to have a little fun. Make that a *ton* of fun: Humpbacks can fly ten feet (3 m) into the air!

4

3

EARNING ITS STRIPES

These **blue stripes** may look like they've been painted on, but they are 100 percent natural. The base of this 'berg highlights how wind and waves can sculpt striking patterns in the ice. But this doesn't occur overnight: It can take hundreds—and sometimes thousands—of years to get such a remarkable effect.

5

SLIP 'N' SLIDE

Who needs a sled when you've got such a smooth belly? **Adélie penguins** sometimes slide—or "toboggan"—across icy ground. Getting an extra push from its flippers and feet, a tobogganing Adélie can reach speeds as fast as humans can run!

ICY CLIFFS

The **Ross Ice Shelf,** a floating sheet of ice covering an area about the size of France, is one of the most stunning sights in Antarctica. At the edges it rises 200 feet (61 m) above sea level, but considering it's up to 6,000 feet (1.8 km) thick in some parts, most of this monster lies underwater.

6

8

SPOT ON

Think this seal looks friendly? Think again. **Leopard seals**—named for their black spotted coats—are some of the fiercest predators in Antarctica. With powerful jaws and extra-long teeth, these sneaky seals primarily prey on penguins, birds, squid, and fish.

7

COLOSSAL CHUNK

The waters around Antarctica are dotted with **icebergs** of all shapes, which form when chunks of ice break off— or calve—from glaciers. These big 'bergs are like floating cities, some measuring larger than the state of Rhode Island, U.S.A., and soaring up to seven stories high.

TURN THE PAGE TO DISCOVER MORE!

WHEN ICEBERGS FLIP!

SEEING BLUE

After a massive iceberg flipped in Antarctica recently, people around the world were stunned to see photos of the underbelly of the 'berg. Jutting out of the water, the jagged formation of deep blue-green colored ice had a polished surface as shiny as a gemstone. The sight was breathtaking.

But, as it turns out, the underwater portion of an iceberg is typically blue or green in color—you just don't see it until it flips.

So where do icebergs get their blue hue? It all has to do with tiny bubbles in the frozen water. These bubbles typically scatter light in every direction and make an iceberg look white. But when that ice melts, water fills cracks in the ice, and then freezes fast enough that no bubbles appear, blue stripes can form, growing deeper in color as the iceberg ages. Also, over the years, 'bergs collect minerals and organic matter in the ocean, giving them such a stunning blue-green shade.

They're massive mountains of ice that soar hundreds of feet (meters) above the surface and can cover as much area as major cities. But as gigantic as some icebergs are, they can also be unstable in the water and vulnerable to flipping. In Antarctica—where there are more icebergs than anywhere else on Earth—capsizing icebergs are not entirely uncommon, though their flipping causes major waves in more ways than one.

So what causes icebergs to roll upside down? Blame gravity—and global warming. When an iceberg forms and plunges into the water, the block of ice is prone to move. And as water and air temperatures rise, the melting 'berg becomes even more unstable, causing its weight distribution to shift. In just a few minutes, the enormous object can completely invert, revealing an untouched underside of ice that's been lurking beneath the surface for thousands of years.

And although it may take just minutes for an iceberg to flip, the effects of the roll can last a lot longer. In fact, scientists say the force of a flip is so strong that some can be compared to a magnitude 5 earthquake or even an atomic bomb explosion. And the result can be tsunami-like monster waves that endanger nearby boats and towns. That's one forceful flip!

EIGHT UNBELIEVABLE ADVENTURES

IT'S A GIANT WORLD OUT THERE—WITH SO MUCH TO DO AROUND EVERY CORNER OF THE EARTH. HERE ARE SOME BEYOND-COOL ACTIVITIES TO UNDERTAKE IN THE GREAT OUTDOORS.

2

JUST DUNE IT
Legend says that the sport of **sandboarding** started in ancient Egypt, where pharaohs slid down dunes on pieces of wood. Today, you can dune it up everywhere from Dubai to down under.

1

NO STRINGS ATTACHED
Climb at your own risk: In **free-climbing**, you use only your hands and feet to scale cliffs and rock walls. Ropes are sometimes used, but only to stop a fall.

3

THE AIR UP THERE
What to do when you're climbing a mountain and need to call it a night? You set up a tent on the rock wall and hit the hay. Special tents called **portaledges** offer secure places to sleep, even if you're 1,500 feet (457 m) up.

WALK THE LINE

In Yosemite National Park in California, U.S.A., a person practices the delicate art of **slacklining,** in which you balance on a bouncy, one-inch (2.5-cm)-wide nylon webbing strung between two rocks.

5

RAPID DESCENT

Look out below! Some **kayakers** get their kicks by plummeting off the top of water-falls. One pro recently launched himself off 186-foot (57-m)-tall falls—then paddled away in one piece.

GET UP, STAND UP

Cowabunga! This **stand-up paddler** propels himself through the water. What started out as simply a quick and efficient way for surfers to paddle out to waves has now emerged into its very own sport, with stand-up paddling races taking place around the world.

6

7

ZIP IT

A visitor to an Ecuadorian rain forest gets a bird's-eye view by **zip-lining** above the trees' canopy. Zip-lining is a thrill-ing way to take in amazing views of the Amazon, especially while safely strapped to a harness attached to a cable.

A PAIR OF MOUNTAIN CLIMBERS RECENTLY REACHED THE TOP OF EL CAPITAN'S DAWN WALL IN YOSEMITE NATIONAL PARK, SCALING 3,000 VERTICAL FEET (914 M) WITHOUT ANY CLIMBING EQUIPMENT.

8

FROZEN FEAT

Baby, it's cold outside, but that doesn't stop **ice climbers** from bundling up and scaling frozen waterfalls and ice caves, like the one here in Tongass National Forest in Alaska, U.S.A.

WHAT: Conrad Maldives
WHERE: Rangali Island, Maldives
WHY IT'S COOL: Set on two remote islands only reachable by a 30-minute seaplane flight, guests can dine at the world's first undersea restaurant while watching whale sharks, manta rays, dolphins, and turtles swim by.

1

EIGHT
HAUGHTIEST HOTELS

FORGET FIVE STARS: THESE SWANKY SPOTS' RATINGS ARE OVER THE MOON. ONCE YOU CHECK IN TO ANY OF THESE HIGH-END HOTELS, YOU MAY NEVER WANT TO LEAVE.

2

WHAT: Attrap' Rêves Hotel
WHERE: Marseille, France
WHY IT'S COOL: Be one with nature without roughing it by staying in one of these inflatable plastic bubbles. Soak up the sun, take a hike, check out the stars through a telescope, and then tuck into your tent for the night. No bug spray required!

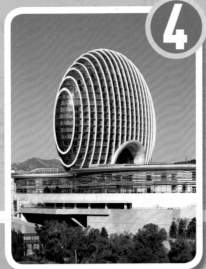

WHAT: Sunrise East Kempinski Hotel
WHERE: Yanqi Lake, China
WHY IT'S COOL: Covered with more than 10,000 glass panels illuminated by LED lights at night, this modern marvel is meant to represent the rising sun over Yanqi Lake.

4

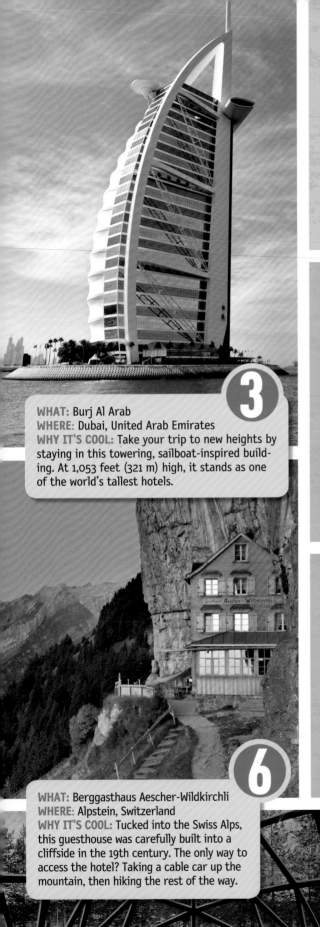

WHAT: Burj Al Arab
WHERE: Dubai, United Arab Emirates
WHY IT'S COOL: Take your trip to new heights by staying in this towering, sailboat-inspired building. At 1,053 feet (321 m) high, it stands as one of the world's tallest hotels.

3

WHAT: Panchoran Retreat
WHERE: Ubud, Bali, Indonesia
WHY IT'S COOL: This nature-inspired retreat features a bamboo bridge perched high over a river and "hideaway bales" where you can do yoga, read, relax, or even have a nap.

5

WHAT: Ice Hotel
WHERE: Jukkasjärvi, Sweden
WHY IT'S COOL: Crafted from ice and snow, the Ice Hotel is rebuilt each year by visiting artists. Layer on the long underwear and *chill* in your suite, which includes a bed made of ... you guessed it: a solid block of ice.

7

WHAT: Berggasthaus Aescher-Wildkirchli
WHERE: Alpstein, Switzerland
WHY IT'S COOL: Tucked into the Swiss Alps, this guesthouse was carefully built into a cliffside in the 19th century. The only way to access the hotel? Taking a cable car up the mountain, then hiking the rest of the way.

6

ONE MEXICAN RESORT OFFERS POSH PUPS SPA SERVICES LIKE MASSAGES AND THEIR OWN DOGGIE CABANA BY THE POOL.

8

WHAT: Kakslauttanen Arctic Resort
WHERE: Saariselkä, Finland
WHY IT'S COOL: Stay in your very own glass igloo and soak up the amazing views of the northern lights each night. Although the igloo is insulated with thermal glass walls, you can stay extra warm in your personal sauna.

EIGHT
PECULIAR PLANTS

PUT ON YOUR GARDENING GLOVES AND DIG IN TO SOME OF THE STINKIEST, SLIMIEST, AND WEIRDEST-LOOKING PLANTS ON EARTH.

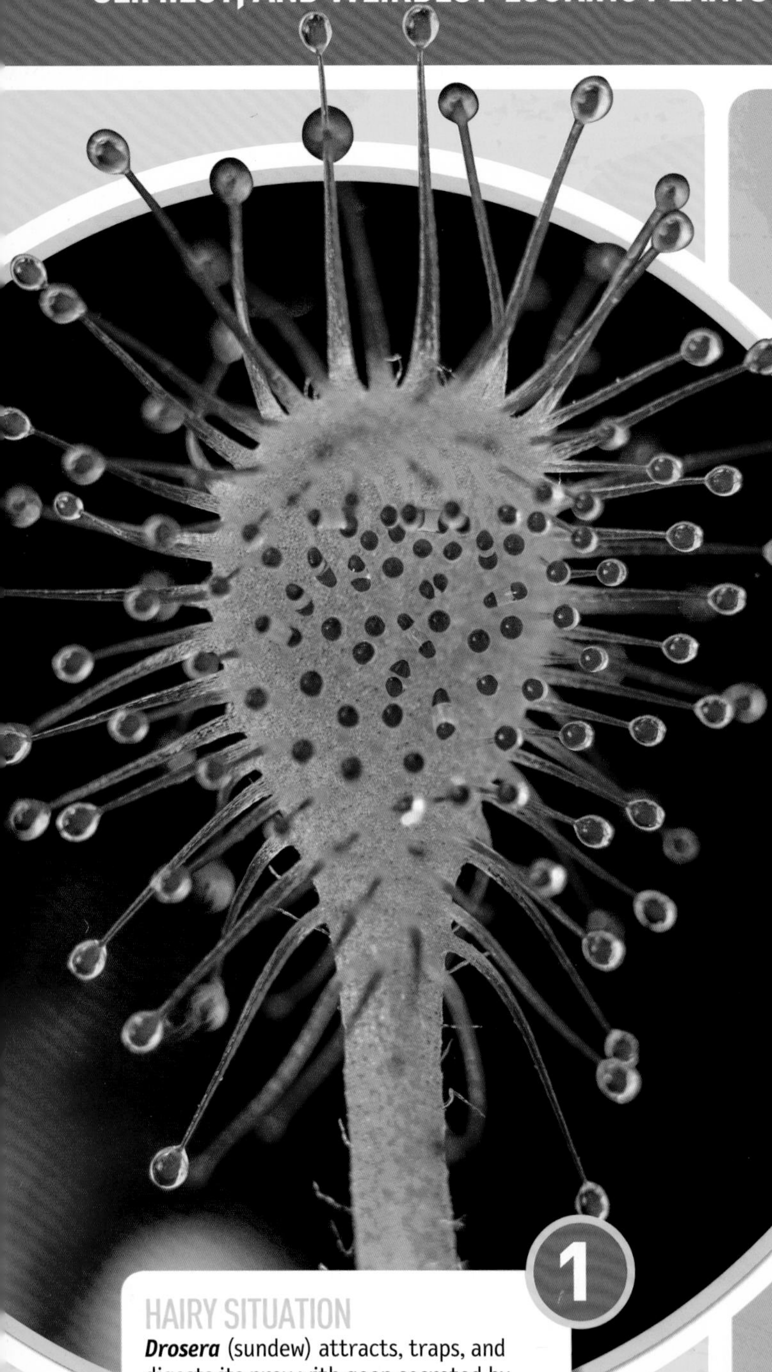

TOWERING STINK

2

True to its nickname, the "corpse flower" emits a rotting-flesh-like smell that helps to attract its pollinators—including dung and carrion beetles—from far away. In its native tropical rain forest habitat, **titan arum** can grow to be 12 feet (3.7 m) tall and weigh as much as 170 pounds (77 kg)!

HAIRY SITUATION

1

Drosera (sundew) attracts, traps, and digests its prey with goop secreted by glands at the end of its long tentacles. A stuck insect is doomed within minutes, but it can take the hairy-looking carnivorous plant up to a few weeks to digest it.

BAT FLOWER

3

Tacca chantrieri earned its creepy common name because of its bat-shaped purplish black flowers. A native of Southeast Asia, this plant—also sometimes called "devil flower"—sports long catlike "whiskers" that drop down from the flower.

BLEEDING TOOTH FUNGUS

Young fruit bodies of **Hydnellum peckii** "bleed" a thick, bright-red fluid when they are damp. Despite its slightly sickly appearance, this fungus—found widely in North America and Europe—is not known to be poisonous.

4

BUDDHA'S HAND

Is it a squid? Or a contorted orange? It's **Citrus medica,** a citrus variety whose fruit is divided into sections, making it look like the long fingers of a human hand.

6

SMELLS LIKE *WHAT?*

Most of the curious **Hydnora africana** plant keeps a low profile, growing underground and out of sight. Its upper portion, however, is hard to miss: It breaks through the ground and gives off the odor of poop to attract its pollinators, including carrion beetles (pictured inside).

7

VOODOO LILY

Also called the **"stink lily," "devil's tongue,"** and **"dragonwort,"** this pretty purple plant—which gives off the smell of rotten meat when it is ready for pollination—may not be the best choice for your valentine bouquet.

8

BIG BLOOM

The rare **Rafflesia arnoldii** has no visible leaves, roots, or stem, but it is the largest known individual flower in the world—able to grow three feet (1 m) across and up to 15 pounds (6.8 kg).

1
SEE-THROUGH SQUID
You can find this balloon-shaped, big-eyed **glass squid** in deep ocean waters of the Southern Hemisphere.

A RESEARCHER ONCE DESCRIBED BEING IN A SWARM OF SEA SALP LIKE "SWIMMING THROUGH A POOL OF JELLY BALLS."

CLEARLY **COOL** CREATURES

YOU DON'T HAVE X-RAY VISION! THESE SEE-THROUGH ANIMALS JUST HAVE NOTHING TO HIDE.

2
QUICK-CHANGE ARTIST
Reversible color change is an unusual ability for an insect, so it's pretty amazing that the **golden tortoise beetle** can quickly change color when disturbed or distressed by predators. The North American insect averages around a quarter of an inch (0.6 cm) in length.

FLAPPING MARVEL

3

The transparent wings of **glasswing butterflies** barely reflect any light, which instead passes through their wing tissue. Their low reflectiveness helps glasswings avoid the clutches of predatory birds, who have a hard time tracking the butterflies during flight.

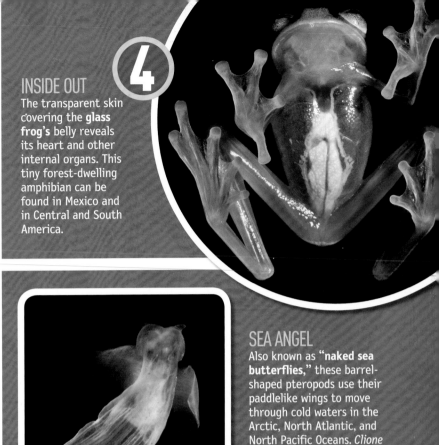

INSIDE OUT

4

The transparent skin covering the **glass frog's** belly reveals its heart and other internal organs. This tiny forest-dwelling amphibian can be found in Mexico and in Central and South America.

SEA ANGEL

5

Also known as **"naked sea butterflies,"** these barrel-shaped pteropods use their paddlelike wings to move through cold waters in the Arctic, North Atlantic, and North Pacific Oceans. *Clione limacina* are born male but can change to be female at some point in their life span.

CRITICAL CRUSTACEAN

6

Shrimplike **krill** may be small in size, but they are hugely important to the food chain. Hundreds of animals worldwide—including whales, fish, and birds—rely on the tiny two-inch (5-cm) ocean-dweller as a staple of their diets.

COMB ON OVER

7

Rows of cilia—the "combs"—on the **comb jelly's** gelatinous exterior work in unison to move it through the water.

JELLY(LIKE) FISH

8

On their own, they're pretty harmless. But a large number of **sea salps** can wreak havoc! A nuclear power plant on the U.S.A.'s central California coast once had to be temporarily shut down after a mass of slimy salps clogged the screens used to keep out marine life.

SEA SALPS CLONE THEMSELVES WHEN THEY ENCOUNTER A "BLOOM" (A LOT) OF THEIR DESIRED PREY.

EIGHT
TRICKY PICS

THESE PHOTOS ARE ALMOST TOO AMAZING TO BE REAL, BUT THEY DEFINITELY ARE! FIND OUT HOW PHOTOGRAPHERS CAPTURE THESE STUNNING SHOTS. NO PHOTOSHOP NECESSARY!

HEAD GAMES
This boy has really **lost his head!** Or it just looks that way as two kids team up for this silly snap. Next time you're at the beach, try to re-create this on your own!

TAPPED OUT
This fountain in Ypres, Belgium, may look like it's **suspended in air.** But what you cannot see is a clear pipe obscured by the falls, funneling water back up to create the illusion of a floating faucet.

WHY SO WOBBLY?
This building in Paris, France, looks like it could belong in a Salvador Dalí **surrealist painting.** The distorted image is actually a reflection in a mirrored covering placed over another building being renovated across the street.

IN THE CLOUDS

This city in the clouds is actually Dubai, United Arab Emirates. The eerie image is the result of a **blanket of fog** floating over the city's skyscrapers.

5

4

FLIPPING OUT

This man appears to be walking on a **very narrow sidewalk.** He flipped things around by lying sideways on the ground. So sneaky.

6

THE PERFECT STORM

It seems like the **weather is a bit confused** when a funnel cloud, a rainbow, and hail hit at once. Although rare, rainbows sometimes do appear during a tornado when slivers of sunlight in the sky reflect off the raindrops.

7

A LEG UP

What long legs you have! A professional soccer player looks as if he has a **superhuman limb** as he warms up for a game. Look closely, though, and you'll see that it's simply an optical illusion created by the player's proximity to his teammates.

8

SPOON MAN

Is this the **world's tiniest man,** or the world's biggest spoon? Actually, it's neither—just the result of a photography trick called forced perspective, an optical illusion that makes objects look bigger or smaller than they actually are.

THE WORLD'S FIRST PHOTOGRAPH WAS TAKEN IN 1826 BY A FRENCH SCIENTIST.

1

BIRD'S NEST

Beijing National Stadium was designed as the main stadium of the 2008 Olympic Games in Beijing, China. This elliptical structure of latticelike strips of steel can hold 91,000 spectators.

EIGHT

BUILDINGS OF THE FUTURE

YES, IT'S REAL! JAW-DROPPING, FUTURISTIC STRUCTURES CAN BE FOUND IN CITIES AND TOWNS ALL OVER THE WORLD.

2

REFLECTING COOL

The **Museum of Contemporary Art (MOCA)** in Cleveland, Ohio, U.S.A., has a hexagonal base and mirror-finish black stainless-steel panels on its exterior, which look different depending on the lighting and the weather conditions.

4
SOARING SKYSCRAPER
It's the tallest building on the planet! The 2,717-foot (828-m) **Burj Khalifa** in Dubai, United Arab Emirates, also features an elevator with the longest travel distance and the highest number of stories (160) in the world.

5
WAVY SPACE
An office and retail complex with more than 3.5 million square feet (325,160 sq m) of floor area in central Beijing, China, **Galaxy SOHO** is a reimagining of a classical Chinese courtyard.

3
WITH A TWIST
The 623-foot (190-m), 54-story **Turning Torso** in Malmö, Sweden, is the country's tallest residential building. It twists 90 degrees from top to bottom (like a person twisting the upper body) and is powered by renewable energy.

7
MARVELOUS METAL
Without a clearly defined shape, the **Ordos Museum**—a center of history and culture in Inner Mongolia, China—seems to move and swell on its own.

6
WATERFRONT WONDER
One of several buildings in the Tjuvholmen Icon Complex on the waterfront in Oslo, Norway, the **Astrup Fearnley Museum of Modern Art** features a glass roof and art spaces linked by a bridge.

READY FOR TAKEOFF
Space-tourism companies (see page 69) can try out their designs and conduct test flights at **Spaceport America,** an otherworldly-looking facility in the Jornada del Muerto desert basin in New Mexico, U.S.A.

8

BONE-CHILLING CHOMPERS

WHAT BIG TEETH YOU HAVE! THESE ANIMALS ARE KNOWN FOR THEIR KILLER BITES.

2 SHARP SPIKES

With a mouthful of spiky teeth and a superflexible jaw, an **anglerfish** can swallow other fish and squid twice its size! Its teeth are also angled inward, helping lock in prey in an instant.

ANGLER-FISH HAVE SEE-THROUGH TEETH.

1 FIERCE FANGS

Boasting the biggest teeth among all land carnivores, a **tiger's** front fangs—called canines—can grow nearly as long as a crayon. Shorter, sharper teeth are prime for keeping prey in place.

3 GREAT BITE

Great whites have several rows of up to 300 sawlike teeth, each of which serves a different function—crushing food, grasping slippery prey, or shredding its victims.

TOTALLY TOXIC

The **king cobra** renders its prey helpless by injecting it with venom through an opening in its hollow fangs. The poison is so strong it can cause a victim's heart to stop in seconds.

5

4

LIP SERVICE

This rare **squid** may seem to have a full set of teeth in its mouth. But what look like neat rows of pearly whites are actually lips that cover its beak.

6

OUT FOR BLOOD

After sinking its long, razorlike fangs into its prey, the **vampire bat—** which is only about the size of your thumb—laps up blood from animals like cows and horses.

7

BIG MOUTH

A **hippo's** huge mouth—it can measure up to four feet (1.2 m) wide!—is filled with massive teeth. Its curved canines never stop growing and can be as long as your leg.

8

SHRED IT

A **crocodile** can't chew: Instead, it uses those cone-shaped chompers and extra-powerful jaws to grasp its prey and tear away the meat before swallowing it in large chunks.

1

WHAT: Fish Building
WHERE: Hyderabad, India
WHY IT'S RIDICULOUS:
Fittingly, this fish-shaped office building is home to India's National Fisheries Development Board.

EIGHT

RIDICULOUS ROADSIDE **ATTRACTIONS**

HIT THE BRAKES! YOU'LL DEFINITELY WANT TO MAKE A PIT STOP AT THESE PECULIAR PLACES FOUND AROUND THE WORLD.

2

WHAT: UFO House
WHERE: Chattanooga, Tennessee, U.S.A.
WHY IT'S RIDICULOUS:
This flying saucer house may not be able to get into orbit, but it does have a front staircase that lowers and retracts with the push of a button—just like a real spaceship.

WHAT: Giant Croc
WHERE: Northern Territory, Australia
WHY IT'S RIDICULOUS: Built to celebrate Australia's victory in a sailing race back in 1983, this boxing croc named Humpty Doo looms nearly two stories above a gas station along a highway.

4

3

WHAT: Straw Big Ben
WHERE: Cheshire, England
WHY IT'S RIDICULOUS: It took 500 bales of straw to create this seven-story replica of London's Big Ben, complete with a working clock that lights up at night.

5

WHAT: Ghost Town
WHERE: Nothing, Arizona, U.S.A.
WHY IT'S RIDICULOUS: This town lives up to its name: With a population of zero, all you'll find here are the remains of an abandoned gas station and convenience store.

6

WHAT: Ball of String
WHERE: Cawker City, Kansas, U.S.A.
WHY IT'S RIDICULOUS: Weighing nearly 20,000 pounds (9,072 kg) and spanning some 41 feet (12.5 m) around, this behemoth ball contains enough twine to wrap around the Epcot "ball" at Walt Disney World 15,000 times!

WHAT: Sheep Building
WHERE: Tirau, New Zealand
WHY IT'S RIDICULOUS: *Baaa!* The site of the Big Sheep Wool Gallery is shaped like the fluffy farm animals, which actually outnumber people in New Zealand.

7

WHAT: Shoe House
WHERE: Hellam, Pennsylvania, U.S.A.
WHY IT'S RIDICULOUS: First built as an advertisement for a shoe company salesman, this five-story boot also has a shoe-shaped doghouse in the yard.

8

EIGHT

DREAM HOMES

COME ON IN! FROM MASSIVE MANSIONS TO EDGY, ARTSY ABODES, YOU'LL FEEL RIGHT AT HOME IN THESE INCREDIBLE DWELLINGS.

ONE 21-BEDROOM BEACHFRONT HOME IN NEW YORK IS SO BIG IT HAS ITS OWN ON-SITE POWER SUPPLY.

1 ROUNDED OUT

Step inside the **Bubble House** in Cannes, France, and you may feel like you're going to float away. This one-of-a-kind, 28-room residence has curved walls and circular windows and beds to really round out the bubble motif.

2 LIVING GREEN

Live the green life in **zeroHouse**, an eco-friendly, prefabricated house that can be built wherever you want. Solar panels on the outside of the house suck up sunlight and convert it to energy, while containers outside collect rain to provide running water.

5

WHEELY COOL

A pro skateboarder designed this house in Malibu, California, U.S.A., so he **can skate everywhere** inside—including on the wooden walls, the curved chairs, the countertops, and even along tubes on the ceiling.

4

CLOUD COVER

The front of this place may look like a nice, ordinary home in Melbourne, Australia. But head to the **cloud-shaped room** in back and you'll see that it's anything but down-to-earth! The ultramodern space is encased in shiny metal, giving this cloud its own silver lining.

8

REVVED UP

This **car-shaped home** in Salzburg, Austria, is an ode to the Volkswagen Beetle. It features separate living areas for kids and adults, a spiral staircase, and energy-efficient heating and cooling systems. As for the headlights? Those are actually windows!

7

FLIP OUT

No, this photo isn't upside down—the house is! A team of architects built this trippy house as a tourist attraction in Terfens, Austria. **Everything is inverted**—down to the car in the garage.

3

BARCODE HOUSE

The residents of this ubercool home in Washington, D.C., are almost always on display, thanks to completely see-through, two-story glass windows. Black steel rods running across the windows **have the look of a bar code**, giving the house its unique nickname.

6

BRICK-TASTIC

Call it the ultimate Lego project: This two-story home and all of its furnishings are made out of **3.3 million Legos**, including a working toilet and shower. It took a team of a thousand volunteers to lock this house in Surrey, England, into place.

INDEX

Boldface indicates illustrations.

PHOTO CREDITS

AL: Alamy; ASP: Alamy Stock Photo; CO: Corbis; DRMS: Dreamstime.com; GI: Getty Images; IS: iStockphoto; MP: Minden Pictures; NC: Newscom; NGC: National Geographic Creative; SS: Shutterstock

Cover (UP LE), AnnaOmelchenko/DRMS; (LO LE), Isselee/DRMS; (CTR), Adrien Veczan/GetStock.com/NC; (UP RT), Fred Bavendam/MP; (CTR RT), Westend61/Kai Jabs/NC; (LO RT), Israel Antiquities Authority Xinhua News Agency/NC; **spine**, Isselee/DRMS; **back cover** (UP RT), Mavrick/DRMS; (CTR LE), GI/Vetta; (LO LE), RudyBalasko/IS; (LO CTR), iStock.com/chuckrasco; 1, Eduard Kyslynskyy/SS; 2-3, Alex Cornell; 4 (UP CTR), outcast85/SS; 4 (CTR LE), Michael Clark/ASP; 4 (LO LE), Lunamarina/DRMS; 4 (CTR RT), NASA; 4 (LO RT), Reinhard Dirscherl/GI; 6 (LE), Dreamworld; 6 (UP RT), Haruyoshi Yamaguchi/CO; 6 (LO RT), Pietro Scozzari/www.agefotostock.com; 7 (UP LE), Oleksiy Maksymenko Photography/ASP; 7 (LO LE), UPPA/Photoshot; 7 (UP RT), Marc Chapeaux/www.agefotostock.com; 7 (CTR RT), Rob DeLorenzo/Zuma Press/NC; 7 (LO RT), Six Flags; 8 (UP), Mike Theiss/NGC; 8 (LO), Grafissimo/IS; 9 (UP LE), IdealPhoto30/IS; 9 (CTR LE), sculpies/IS; 9 (LO LE), Michael Melford/NGC; 9 (UP RT), Paul Chesley/NGC; 9 (CTR RT), Vincent J. Musi/NGC; 9 (LO RT), Tino Soriano/NGC; 10, Andreanita/DRMS; 11 (UP LE), Reinhard Dirscherl/GI; 11 (CTR), Mrdoomits/DRMS; 11 (CTR LE), Plunne/DRMS; 11 (LO CTR), iStock.com/Carima van den Berg; 11 (LO LE), Kikkerdirk/DRMS; 11 (UP RT), Karen Gowlett-Holmes/GI; 11 (LO RT), Surz01/DRMS; 12-13, Image Source/ASP; 13 (UP LE), Vitalii Hulai/SS; 13 (LO LE), EcoPrint/SS; 13 (UP RT), Mark Newman/GI; 13 (LO RT), imageBROKER/ASP; 14 (UP), Splash/Hammacher Schlemmer/Newscom; 14 (LO), Arno Burgi/EPA/NC; 15 (A), Terrafugia; 15 (B), Terrafugia; 15 (C), Enis Balibouse/POOL/EPA/NC; 15 (D), Eduardo Galvani/Rex/REX USA; 15 (E), Fabrice Coffrini/AFP/GI; 15 (F), David Erickson/Ravalli Republic; 15 (G), David Erickson/Ravalli Republic; 15 (H), GH1/wenn.com/NC; 16 (LE), Marius Bøstrand; 16 (UP RT), Michael Clark/ASP; 16 (LO RT), EPA/NC; 17 (UP LE), Anthony Devlin/PA Wire; 17 (CTR LE), AP Photo/Channi Anand; 17 (UP RT), Bigfoot Hostel/Barcroft Media/GI; 17 (CTR RT), Lucas Jackson/Reuters; 17 (LO), Pictures Colour Library/NC; 18 (UP), Robinson/REX SS; 18 (LO), zumapress.com/NC; 19 (UP LE), Mike Clarke/AFP/GI; 19 (CTR LE), Ray Tang/REX SS; 19 (UP RT), Philippe Hays/REX SS; 19 (CTR RT UP), AquaOne Technologies; 19 (CTR RT LO), Okauchi/REX SS; 19 (LO), MCT/NC; 20 (LE), All Canada Photos/ASP; 20 (UP RT), Bayda127/DRMS; 20 (LO RT), Poutnik/DRMS; 21 (UP LE), Bbbar/DRMS; 21 (CTR LE), Mavrick/DRMS; 21 (UP RT), Mauro77photo/DRMS; 21 (CTR RT), Csterken/DRMS; 21 (LO), Lunamarina/DRMS; 22 (BKGD), Lauren G. Fields; 23 (A), Sascha Grabow/Ocean/CO; 23 (B), Design Pics/NC; 23 (C), Marvin Vetter/Oregon Dept. of Forestry/USDA; 23 (D), Daniel L. Osborne/Detlev van Ravenswaa/Science Source; 23 (E), OAR/ERL/National Severe Storms Laboratory (NSSL)/NOAA; 23 (F), Mike Lyvers/GI; 23 (G), Natalia Bratslavsky/SS; 24-25 (BKGD), GIPhotoStock/Science Source/GI; 25 (LE), Richard D. Norris; 25 (RT), Sven Sjöström/EyeEm/GI; 26 (UP), Richard Jones/Sinopix/Rex Features; 26 (LO), Design Pics Inc/NGC; 27 (UP LE), Andrea Comas/Reuters; 27 (CTR LE), Janossy Gergely/SS; 27 (UP RT), outcast85/SS; 27 (CTR RT), iStock.com/eve_eve-01genesis; 27 (CTR), Stefanie van der Vinden/SS; 27 (LO RT), Katherine Feng/Globio/MP/NGC; 28 (LE), AP Photo/Bonhams; 28 (UP RT), James L. Amos/NGC; 28 (LO RT), Jason Dunlop; 29 (UP LE), Phil Degginger/Carnegie Museum/AL; 29 (CTR LE), Colin Keates/DK Limited/CO; 29 (UP RT), Pierre-Oliver Antoine; 29 (CTR RT), Heritage Auctions/Rex USA; 29 (LO), Calvert Marine Museum/Barcroft Media/GI; 30 (BKGD), Yuri Yavnik/SS; 31 (A), Angelo Hornak/AL; 31 (B), Christian Kober/GI; 31 (C), S.R. Lee Photo Traveller/SS; 31 (D), ARCO/Lenz G/www.agefotostock.com; 31 (E), James L. Stanfield/NGC; 31 (F), Graeme Peacock/AL; 31 (G), Sebastian Nicolae/SS; 32-33 (BKGD), Emi Cristea/SS; 33 (UP RT), iStock.com/Ivan Bliznetsov; 33 (CTR RT), iStock.com/Michael Powers; 33 (CTR LE), Mary Evans Picture Library/ASP; 33 (LO RT), imageBROKER/ASP; 34 (UP), Caters News Agency; 34 (LO), Lucy Gauntlett; 35 (UP LE), Alasdair Jardine; 35 (CTR LE), Tom Hare-artist, Daniel Castledine-photographer; 35 (LO LE), CB2/ZOB/wenn.com/NC; 35 (UP RT), CB2/ZOB/wenn.com/NC; 35 (CTR RT), Masaya Yoshimura/Daici Ano; 35 (LO RT), Caters News Agency; 36 (UP), Rinusbaak/DRMS; 36 (LO), Yadid Levy/AL; 37 (UP LE), GI/Vetta; 37 (CTR LE), Ulana Switucha/AL; 37 (UP RT), Richard Ellis/GI; 37 (CTR RT), Andy Buchanan/AFP/GI; 37 (CTR), David Ramos/GI; 37 (LO), epa european pressphoto agency b.v./AL; 38 (LE), Ray Tang/REX SS; 38 (UP RT), UPI/NC; 38 (LO RT), Splash News/NC; 39 (UP LE), Richard Graulich/The Palm Beach Post/Zuma Wire; 39 (CTR LE), CB2/ZOB/wenn.com/NC; 39 (UP RT), Kieran Dodds/REX SS; 39 (CTR RT), Cavendish Press/Splash News; 39 (LO RT), NC; 40 (UP), Thomas Boehm/AL; 40 (LO), Mirrorpix/NC; 41 (UP LE), Brian Pickell; 41 (CTR LE), Heritage Image Partnership Ltd/AL; 41 (LO LE), View Pictures Ltd via NC; 41 (UP RT), Gordon Sinclair/AL; 41 (CTR), Jay C. Easton; 41 (LO RT), The Toronto Star/Zuma Press; 42 (LE), AP Photo/Fresno Bee, Tomas Ovalle; 42 (UP RT), Junko Kimura/Jana Press/zumapress.com; 42 (LO RT), Jussi Nukari/REX SS; 43 (UP LE), Danny Martindale/GI; 43 (CTR LE), Evan Agostini/Invision/AP; 43 (UP RT), GI/Helene Wiesenhaan; 43 (CTR RT), Mulholland/REX SS; 43 (LO), Alex Milan Tracy/SIPA USA/NC; 44 (BKGD), Carsten Peter/NGC; 45 (UP LE), MCT via GI; 45 (CTR UP), Stephen Frink Collection/ASP; 45 (CTR LE), Balint Porneczi/Bloomberg via GI; 45 (CTR LO), iStock.com/Cameron Strathdee; 45 (LO LE), Clavel/AFP/GI; 45 (UP RT), Mark Thiessen/NGC; 45 (LO RT), Carsten Peter/NGC; 46-47 (BKGD), Arctic-Images/CO; 46 (LO LE), Arctic Images/ASP; 46 (UP RT), Nigel Sawyer/ASP; 46 (LO RT), Arctic Images/ASP; 47 (UP RT), Arctic-Images/CO; 48 (UP), Jon Hughes/DK Images/GI; 48 (LO), Richard Nowitz/NGC; 49 (UP LE), Stocktrek Images, Inc./AL; 49 (CTR LE), blickwinkel/AL; 49 (LO LE), Roger Harris/Science Source; 49 (UP RT), blickwinkel/AL; 49 (CTR RT), Leonello Calvetti/Stocktrek Images/CO; 49 (LO RT), Dennis Hallinan/AL; 50 (UP), travel images/AL; 50 (LO), Heng Sinith/epa/CO; 51 (A), Neil Setchfield/AL; 51 (B), Food and Drink Photos/AL; 51 (C), Tobias Titz/fstop/CO; 51 (D), Suzy Bennett/AL; 51 (E), Jessica Boschen; 51 (F), National Park Service; 51 (G), Giuseppe Viterale; 51 (H), Tosh Brown/AL; 52 (LE), NASA, ESA, J. Hester and A. Loll (Arizona State University); 52 (UP RT), NASA and The Hubble Heritage Team (STScI/AURA); 52 (LO RT), NASA; 53 (UP LE), NASA, H. Ford (JHU), G. Illingworth (UCSC/LO), M.Clampin (STScI), G. Hartig (STScI), the ACS Science Team, and ESA; 53 (CTR LE), NASA, ESA, and The Hubble Heritage Team (STScI/AURA); 53 (UP RT), NASA, ESA, and E. Karkoschka (University of Arizona); 53 (CTR RT), NASA; 53 (LO), NASA, ESA, and The Hubble Heritage Team (STScI/AURA); 54 (UP), Paul Souders/GI; 54 (LO), Dallas and John Heaton/NC; 55 (UP LE), C. Recoura/Versailles-SNCF/SIPA/NC; 55 (CTR LE), Kyodo/NC; 55 (UP RT), Siemens AG Pressebilder/Presspictures; 55 (CTR RT UP), Annebicque Bernard/CO Sygma; 55 (CTR RT LO), Zuma Press/NC; 55 (LO RT), AP Photo/Keystone, Markus Stuecklin; 56 (LE), EPA/NC; 56 (UP RT), AFP/GI; 56 (LO RT), AP Photo/Allen Breed; 57 (UP LE), Randy Duchaine/ASP; 57 (CTR LE), Toshiyuki Aizawa/Reuters; 57 (UP RT), Splash News/NC; 57 (CTR RT), Splash News/NC; 57 (LO), Michael Caronna/Reuters; 58 (UP), Kent Kobersteen/NGC; 58 (LO), Matej Hudovernik/IS; 59 (A), Mario Carvajal; 59 (B), Roger T Wong/GI; 59 (C), Vadim Petrakov/SS; 59 (D), Ockert le Roux; 59 (E), StephanHoerold/IS; 59 (F), Mike Theiss/NGC; 60, Iain Masterton/incamerastock/CO; 61 (UP LE), WENN Ltd/ASP; 61 (CTR), PRNewsFoto/Six Flags Over Georgia; 61 (CTR LE), Therme Erding; 61 (CTR LE LO), WENN Ltd/ASP; 61 (LO LE), WhiteWater World; 61 (UP RT), Mathew Monteith/ASP; 61 (LO RT), Beach Park; 62-63 (BKGD), Macduff Everton/CO; 63 (UP), Therme Erding; 63 (LO), Beach Park; 64 (LE), Mattel, Inc/Splash News/NC; 64 (UP RT), Ezio Petersen UPI Photo Service/NC; 64 (LO RT), Bettmann/CO; 65 (UP LE), John Angelillo/UPI/NC; 65 (CTR LE), JP5/ZOB/wenn.com/NC; 65 (UP RT), Metropolis Collectibles/Comic Connect; 65 (CTR RT), Webb's; 65 (LO), Terry O'Neill/GI; 66 (UP), Dan Bergeron; 66 (LO), Xinhua/eyevine/Redux; 67 (UP LE), Rex Features via AP Images; 67 (CTR LE), oakoak; 67 (LO LE), Rex Features via AP Images; 67 (UP RT), epa european pressphoto agency b.v./AL; 67 (CTR RT), Evening Standard/eyevine/Redux; 67 (LO RT), Mariusz Switulski/SS; 68 (UP), GH1/wenn.com/NC; 68 (LO), RomanBabakin/IS; 69 (A), unimedia-images Inc/Unimedia International/NC; 69 (B), Stephen Hird/Reuters/CO; 69 (C), oksana.perkins/SS; 69 (D), Fomichev Mikhail Itar-Tass Photos/NC; 69 (E), Martin Aircraft Company; 69 (F), Steve Parry; 70 (LE), Jodi Cobb/NGC; 70 (UP RT), Chris Willson/AL; 70 (LO RT), North Wind Picture Archives/The Image Works; 71 (UP LE), The Knohl Collection; 71 (CTR LE), Randy Duchaine/AL; 71 (UP RT), Danita Delimont/Gallo Images/GI; 71 (CTR RT), Walter Meayers Edwards/NGC; 71 (LO), Tom Lovell/NGC; 72 (UP), Hollandse Hoogte/CO; 72 (LO), Peter Brooker/REX SS; 73 (UP LE), Caters News Agency; 73 (CTR LE), MCT/NC; 73 (UP RT), Jim West/ASP; 73 (CTR RT UP), REX SS; 73 (CTR RT LO), CO; 73 (LO RT), www.DanitaDelimont.com/NC; 74 (BKGD), AP Photo/ARGO via Greek Culture Ministry, Brett Seymour; 74 (LO), Aristidis Vafeiadakis/Zuma Press/CO; 75 (A), Victor R. Boswell, Jr/NGC; 75 (B), Xinhua/eyevine/Redux Pictures; 75 (C), Baz Ratner/Reuters/CO; 75 (D), Israel Antiquities Authority Xinhua News Agency/NC; 75 (E), Philip Crummy; 75 (F), Stringer/Reuters/NC; 75 (G), ©Franck Goddio/Hilti Foundation; 76-77 (BKGD), Photo by Christoph Gerigk ©Franck Goddio/Hilti Foundation; 76 (CTR), Photo by Christoph Gerigk ©Franck Goddio/Hilti Foundation; 76 (LO), ©Franck Goddio/Hilti Foundation; 78 (LE), JDMaddox/IS; 78 (UP RT), Stephen Frink/CO; 78 (LO RT), Christian Ziegler/NGC; 79 (UP LE), Dietmar Nill/GI; 79 (CTR LE), Christian Ziegler/NGC; 79 (UP RT), Jim Brandenburg/MP/GI; 79 (CTR RT), Reinhard Dirscherl/GI; 79 (LO), Brent Hedges/Nature Picture Library; 80 (UP), Pep Roig/ASP; 80 (LO), Sean Pavone/ASP; 81 (UP LE), P. Eoche/GI; 81 (CTR LE), Darren McLoughlin/ASP; 81 (LO LE), phillipschip/IS; 81 (UP RT), Freesurf69/DRMS; 81 (CTR RT), Babak Tafreshi/NGC; 81 (LO RT), GI/Flickr RF; 82 (LE), Geoffrey Robinson/Rex/REX USA; 82 (UP RT), Rex/REX USA; 82 (LO RT), Baloncici/DRMS; 83 (UP LE), WENN/NC; 83 (CTR LE), Rex/REX USA; 83 (UP RT), MotorcycleMojo/REX USA; 83 (CTR RT), Caters News Agency; 83 (LO), Solent News/Rex/REX USA; 84 (UP), iStock.com/Johnson; 84 (LO), iStock.com/Richard Whitcombe; 85 (UP LE), iStock.com/Guenter Guni; 85 (CTR LE), Eduard Kyslynskyy/SS; 85 (LO LE), iStock.com/technotr; 85 (UP RT), Chris Johns/NGC; 85 (CTR RT), iStock.com/Andy Astbury; 85 (LO RT), iStock.com/chuckrasco; 86 (UP), NetPlayWorks/Rex Features/Associated Press; 86 (LO), Tiong Bahru Park Playground; 87 (UP LE), LightRocket via GI; 87 (CTR LE), Jose More/VWPics/NC; 87 (UP RT), Amiee Stubbs; 87 (CTR RT UP), C Palma; 87 (CTR RT LO), Citizen of the Planet/ASP; 87 (LO RT), Tony Kyriacou/REX SS; 88, AccentAlaska.com/ASP; 89 (UP LE), Paul Nicklen/NGC; 89 (CTR), iStock.com/Roland Brack; 89 (CTR LE), iStock.com/Flair; 89 (CTR LE LO), Rick Price/GI; 89 (LO LE), Paul Nicklen/NGC; 89 (UP RT), Paul Nicklen/NGC; 89 (LO RT), Jan Vermeer/FN/MP/NGC; 90-91 (BKGD), Alex Cornell; 92 (LE), iStock.com/Vernon Wiley; 92 (UP RT), Extreme Sports Photo/ASP; 92 (LO RT), Jimmy Chin/NGC; 93 (UP LE), iStock.com/MichaelSvoboda; 93 (CTR LE), Skip Brown/NGC; 93 (UP RT), MBI/ASP; 93 (CTR RT), Ammit/ASP; 93 (LO), Design Pics Inc/NGC; 94 (UP), zumapress.com/NC; 94 (UP LE), zumapress.com/NC; 94 (LO), Pochard Pascal/SIPA/NC; 95 (UP LE), Serban Enache/DRMS; 95 (CTR LE), Prisma Bildagentur AG/ASP; 95 (LO), WENN Ltd/ASP; 95 (UP RT), Xing Guangli/NC; 95 (CTR RT), Larry Dale Gordon/ASP; 95 (CTR), Johner/GI; 96 (LE), Alexander Taranukhin; 96 (UP RT), B Christopher/AL; 96 (LO RT), Michael Melford/NGC; 97 (UP LE), DP Wildlife Fungi/AL; 97 (CTR LE), Malcolm Coe/Oxford Scientific/GI; 97 (LO), JapanNature/IS; 97 (UP RT), ADS/AL; 97 (CTR RT), shapencolour/AL; 97 (LO RT), SuperStock/www.agefotostock.com; 98 (UP), Deep-Sea Photography; 98 (LO), Mark Moffett/MP; 99 (A), Frans Lanting/NGC; 99 (B), Visual&Written SL/AL; 99 (C), Pete Oxford/MP; 99 (D), Sonke Johnsen/Visuals Unlimited/CO; 99 (E), George Grall/NGC; 99 (F), Conaugh Fraser/Caters News Agency; 100 (LE), NRT-Helena/ASP; 100 (UP RT), David Trood/GI; 100 (LO RT), DWImages Europe/ASP; 101 (UP LE), GI/Cultura Exclusive; 101 (CTR LE), GI/Photo Researchers RM; 101 (UP RT), GI/Flickr RM; 101 (CTR RT), Jed Leicester/BPI/REX; 101 (LO), Mike Theiss/GI; 102 (UP), Xi Zhang/DRMS; 102 (LO), RaymondBoyd/GI; 103 (A), Dennis Dolkens/DRMS; 103 (B), Kim Carlson/DRMS; 103 (C), Nanisimova/DRMS; 103 (D), Sophiejames/DRMS; 103 (E), View Pictures/UIG via GI; 103 (F), Mitchell Masilun/AL; 103 (G), Zuma Press, Inc/AL; 104 (LE), Sergey Uryadnikov/SS; 104 (UP RT), Sonke Johnsen/Visuals Unlimited/CO; 104 (LO RT), Fred Bavendam/MP; 105 (UP LE), Richard E. Young; 105 (CTR LE), Michael & Patricia Fogden/MP; 105 (UP RT), Martin Harvey/GI; 105 (CTR RT), gianlucabartoli/IS; 105 (LO), Shandhika Chatoor/DRMS; 106 (UP), Exotica/AL; 106 (LO), AP/Photo Mark Gilliland; 107 (UP LE), Andrew Yates/AFP/GI; 107 (CTR LE), Franck Fotos/AL; 107 (LO LE), A. L. Spangler/SS; 107 (UP RT), Christopher Groenhout/GI; 107 (CTR RT), Bryan Mullennix/Spaces Images/CO; 107 (LO RT), Aurora Photos/AL; 108 (UP LE), courtesy of Zero House; 108 (UP RT), courtesy of Zero House; 108 (LO RT), SYSPEO/SIPA/NC; 109 (UP LE), wenn.com/NC; 109 (CTR LE), World Architecture Festival/SIPA/NC; 109 (LO LE), Paul Warchol; 109 (UP RT), action press/NC; 109 (CTR RT), Dominic Ebenbichler/Reuters; 109 (LO RT), UPPA/Photoshot/NC; 112: top, left to right: Orhan Cam/SS; Hotshotsworldwide/DRMS; Bplane/SS; winui/SS; bottom: Sisse Brimberg/NGC

SAD TO SEE THE BOOK END? HERE ARE FIVE QUICK LIGHTNING LISTS TO KEEP THE FUN GOING:

EIGHT AWESOME
SIGHTS TO SEE IN WASHINGTON, D.C.

1. The Washington Monument
2. The White House
3. The Newseum
4. Mount Vernon
   (Washington's home in nearby Alexandria, Virginia)
5. The memorials (all of them!)
6. The Smithsonian museums
7. Georgetown
8. The Old Post Office Pavilion

EIGHT FAVORITE
ANIMALS OF THE NG KIDS STAFF

1. Sloth
2. Koala
3. Dolphin
4. Narwhal
5. Bunny
6. Dog
7. Cat
8. Horse

EIGHT THINGS
THAT HAPPENED IN THE YEAR 1888

1. The National Geographic Society was founded.
2. The first drinking straw was patented.
3. The English Football League was established ("soccer," as it is known in the United States).
4. Frederick Douglass became the first African American nominated for U.S. president.
5. The first electric automobile was unveiled.
6. The first known recording of classical music was made.
7. Jack the Ripper haunted the streets of London, England.
8. The first roll of camera film was invented and the name "Kodak" was patented.

EIGHT GREAT
THINGS ABOUT THE INTERNET

1. The first Tweet was sent in 2006.
2. The first YouTube video was uploaded in 2005.
3. The original website for the movie Space Jam, which came out in 1996, is still live.
4. There's a website with a running counter that updates each day how old the Internet is.
5. The first email was sent in 1971.
6. The Amazon logo contains a hidden message: They have everything from A to Z.
7. The first website is still online.
8. Google uses 1,000 computers to answer queries in 0.2 seconds.

EIGHT BIGGEST
LIBRARIES IN THE WORLD

1. British Library (170 million books), London, England
2. Library of Congress (160 million books), Washington, D.C., U.S.A.
3. Library and Archives Canada (54 million books), Ottowa, Canada
4. New York Public Library (53.1 million books), New York City, U.S.A.
5. Russian State Library (44.4 million books), Moscow, Russia
6. Bibliothèque nationale de France (40 million books), Paris, France
7. National Library of Russia (36.5 million books), St. Petersburg, Russia
8. National Diet Library (35.6 million books), Tokyo and Kyoto, Japan

Copyright © 2016 National Geographic Partners, LLC

Julide Obuz Dengel and Callie Broaddus, *Art Directors*; Nicole Lazarus, *Designer*

All rights reserved. Reproduction of the whole or any part of the contents without written permission from the publisher is prohibited.

Since 1888, the National Geographic Society has funded more than 12,000 research, exploration, and preservation projects around the world. The Society receives funds from National Geographic Partners, LLC, funded in part by your purchase. A portion of the proceeds from this book supports this vital work.

For more information, visit www.natgeo.com/info, call 1-800-647-5463, or write to the following address:
National Geographic Partners, LLC
1145 17th Street N.W.
Washington, D.C. 20036-4688 U.S.A.

Visit us online at nationalgeographic.com/bo

For librarians and teachers: ngchildrensbook

More for kids from National Geographic:
kids.nationalgeographic.com

For information about special discounts for purchases, please contact National Geograph Books Special Sales: ngspecsales@ngs.org

For rights or permissions inquiries, please co
National Geographic Books Subsidiary Rights
ngbookrights@ngs.org

Paperback ISBN: 978-1-4263-2337-9
Reinforced library binding ISBN:
978-1-4263-2338-6

Printed in China
16/RRDS/1